How Administrators
Can Improve Teaching

Peter Seldin and Associates

Foreword by Russell Edgerton

How Administrators
Can Improve Teaching

*Moving from Talk to Action
in Higher Education*

 Jossey-Bass Publishers

San Francisco • Oxford • 1990

HOW ADMINISTRATORS CAN IMPROVE TEACHING
Moving from Talk to Action in Higher Education
by Peter Seldin and Associates

Copyright © 1990 by: Jossey-Bass Inc., Publishers
350 Sansome Street
San Francisco, California 94104
&
Jossey-Bass Limited
Headington Hill Hall
Oxford OX3 0BW

Library of Congress Cataloging-in-Publication Data

How administrators can improve teaching : moving from talk to action
in higher education / Peter Seldin and associates.
    p.   cm. — (The Jossey-Bass higher education series)
  Includes bibliographical references.
  ISBN 1-55542-277-2
  1. College teaching—United States.   2. Universities and colleges—
United States—Administration.   I. Seldin, Peter.   II. Series.
LB2331.H66   1990
378.1′25′0973—dc20   90-34308
                                                                CIP

Manufactured in the United States of America

The paper in this book meets the guidelines for
permanence and durability of the Committee on
Production Guidelines for Book Longevity of the
Council on Library Resources.

JACKET DESIGN BY WILLI BAUM

FIRST EDITION

Code 9070

The Jossey-Bass
Higher Education Series

Contents

ix

Foreword

From students who cannot understand their teaching assistants, parents who want results, and legislators concerned about costs come increasing pressure to improve teaching. The opportunities for making improvements in education are growing. It is estimated that between 1990 and 2004, colleges and universities will hire 335,000 new professors. Educators are being given another opportunity to find new answers to the often-repeated questions: What training should graduate schools provide? What sort of "teaching residency" would get beginning teachers off to the best start? How can we evaluate teachers' performance in a way that takes into account the complexity of teaching?

It is especially timely that Peter Seldin has invited the contributors to this book to address the special role that administrators of colleges and universities can play in improving teaching. The chapter authors include not only scholars of management and education but also reflective practitioners who have personally engineered improvements in teaching and survived to tell the tale. What results is a feast of information and ideas.

Yet precisely because the time is so ripe and the "menu" provided here is so rich, I found myself worrying while reading *How Administrators Can Improve Teaching* that some readers be provided with answers before they ask the necessary questions. For example, a new provost arrives who is committed to "do something" to improve teaching. Then a committee is formed. Next thing you know, there is a new center for teaching improvement, and a program is designed to recognize outstanding teachers. These changes may be just what is needed, but no one really knows, because no one has asked the crucial question: "What is the problem we are trying to solve?"

Each of the contributors to this volume addresses a different problem. For Rice and Austin, the problem lies in the ambiguity of institutional missions; for Green, in the fact that administrators do not view themselves as leaders. Lucas considers the problem to be the woeful preparation of department chairs. Cashin, Menges, and Cross each view the problem as residing with the faculty, who fail to do research on their own teaching or to make use of known techniques for assessing student learning.

I have much enthusiasm for the various courses of action recommended. But I also feel that progress depends on a well-conceived strategy to guide the effort—a strategy based on diagnosis of the deeper sources of the problem. Why do faculty neglect known techniques for improving teaching? Why are department chairs woefully underprepared? Seldin makes this blunt statement in the first chapter: "Teaching is widely undervalued today." But why is this so?

Balancing the Teeter-Totter

The most common answer to this question, which is familiar to us all, is, "Because another activity—research—is so highly valued." Teaching and research are thought of as two children on a teeter-totter: if one is up, the other must be down. The solution that follows from this definition of the problem is that more weight should be given to teaching if teaching is to improve.

Clearly, the issue of balance is important, and there are reasons to believe that progress can be made. A recent survey at Syracuse University showed that most deans and department chairs favored giving teaching a higher priority but thought that their colleagues accorded higher priority to research. Publication of this evidence of wide support for teaching surprised everyone and stirred new interest in achieving a better balance between teaching and research.

However, it would be well not to underestimate how massive are the forces arrayed behind research. A friend who serves on the board of trustees of a "second-tier" liberal arts college recently told me a story that illustrates this point.

The board was considering a policy statement about what teaching work loads would be appropriate in what the president called a "research college." (This term evolved as prestigious liberal arts colleges tried to make the case that they were eligible for federal funds that were newly available for science facilities.) One board member strongly objected to the idea of a research college and to a provision in the policy statement allowing for a reduction in teaching loads. In response, a young faculty member argued, "If this isn't passed, I'll be stuck here for the rest of my life." He pointed out that many "top-tier" liberal arts colleges were reducing their teaching loads.

This college is caught in a system not of its own making and is deeply affected by decisions of other institutions, which are in turn affected by a system of financial incentives that, in this case, date back to the Manhattan Project.

To achieve a better balance of priorities on campus, we must attain a better balance of priorities outside the campus. If all the discretionary dollars in the system are available only for research, it should not be surprising that research gets the attention. The chapter by Chickering and Potter should inspire a new discussion about the actions states might take to begin redressing the balance between teaching and research.

The Reconceptualization of Pedagogy

In addition to being difficult to implement, the strategy of giving more weight to teaching has another limitation—namely, the assumption that teaching is itself a valued commodity. But, in fact, teaching is devalued for other reasons than that priority is given to research. As Sheridan points out in this volume, "Ichabod Crane dies hard." Many faculty members have little respect for teaching as a professional activity. Even those who care deeply about their own teaching and are themselves exemplary teachers often do not regard teaching as an intellectually interesting topic for professional discourse.

For example, consider a tenure review committee in which teaching is emphasized but no one on the committee believes that the evidence presented about a candidate's performance as a teacher is worth much or lends itself to peer evaluation and judgment. Until we diagnose and address why this attitude exists, it will be difficult to improve the status of teaching in a fundamental way.

I am persuaded that one source of this problem is the historical separation of the subjects we teach from the process of teaching. The study of teaching evolved around a paradigm of teaching "in general"—teaching across all fields and disciplines. Hence, when we think about learning to teach, we consider such items as how to make effective presentations, how to lead discussion groups, or how to evaluate student learning. These are indeed basic and necessary skills, but they are not topics that really interest teachers.

In this area, however, changes are being made. In recent years, a number of researchers have provided the intellectual underpinnings for a new view of pedagogy that can capture the imagination of the faculty.

Researchers in the cognitive sciences, for example, have been telling us that learning is domain specific. To put it more simply, students might think abstractly in one subject area and concretely in another. Other researchers have advanced similar arguments about teaching. Lee Shulman at Stanford, for example, has found that exemplary teachers have many techniques—analogies, metaphors, demonstrations—for transforming the ideas they are trying to convey into images their students will understand. These are not general methods but specific ways of representing the ideas of each discipline and field.

All this implies that we need a more contextual conception of pedagogy—a rationale for basing the study and
practice of teaching on what is being taught and to whom.
Would-be teachers need to consider how to lead a good discussion, but they also need to consider what conceptions and
misconceptions their students are likely to bring to a classroom discussion about the concept of, for example, natural
selection and in what multiple ways they can represent such
concepts and relate them to students' particular backgrounds
and experiences. Teaching by context, in my view, is a topic
that can capture faculty attention.

A Strategy for Integration

The implications of this view for promoting teaching
are profound. At issue here is the need not simply to emphasize teaching more but to rethink what teaching is and how
one learns to do it well.

The problem is not simply that graduate schools fail to
prepare students for their role as teachers but that even in
schools where preparation is adequate, teaching is often
regarded as an area separate from what one's chosen field of
interest might be. Teaching is considered by teachers and
administrators as an add-on, not an expression of one's scholarly expertise.

The issue is not simply that first-year teachers do not
get the kind of help they need but that, all too often, the help
available is generalized rather than specific. The difficulty is
not simply that teaching is not rewarded but that, discipline
by discipline, faculty have not assumed responsibility for
thinking of the ways and means that teaching can be peer
reviewed.

What is necessary is a strategy of integration. Although
it is important to balance the dual emphases on teaching and
on research, achieving this balance should not lead us to pit
teaching against research. As we emphasize that being a good
historian, physicist, or chemist is essential, we need to
acknowledge that it is not enough. A historian is not neces-

sarily a good history professor. We must assure our students and our public that each academic department has professors of professional stature who are also good teachers.

For every department to have good professors, academic leaders must know what their roles will be in creating a campus climate that motivates faculty and supports teaching. This book shows administrators how to provide the needed leadership to foster really effective teaching at their institutions. *How Administrators Can Improve Teaching* is a necessary addition to the library of every academic administrator.

July 1990   Russell Edgerton
                                   President, American Association
                                   for Higher Education

Preface

Almost all colleges and universities profess to be committed to effective teaching, as is evident in their brochures and catalogues. Even a cursory examination of these reassures us that the institutions are fervently dedicated to high-quality instruction.

However, this representation is open to challenge from those who teach and those who learn in today's colleges and universities. A disquieting number of faculty and students argue that their personal experience belies the officially stated reverence for teaching. The fact of the matter is that most colleges and universities, despite the rhetoric to the contrary, favor research and scholarly performance over teaching in making recruitment, promotion, and tenure decisions.

Teaching is widely undervalued today. The faculty member more interested in teaching than in scholarly research is soon forced by the institution's reward system to reverse direction. There is some truth to the common notion that professors are paid to teach but are rewarded for research and publication.

Very little in today's campus climate supports improved teaching, which may explain why only small numbers of faculty members participate in programs offered by faculty development centers to improve teaching performance. Why bother to hone teaching skills when the road to promotion and tenure is through research and scholarship? Even professors at the hundreds of nonresearch institutions, where teaching is still supposedly paramount, know the pragmatic importance of developing a scholarly résumé.

However, change may be in the wind. Pressures from such diverse sources as the Carnegie Foundation for the Advancement of Teaching, the American Association for Higher Education, state legislatures, faculty, and students have begun to move some colleges and universities to reconsider the importance of teaching.

How can institutions bring a new professionalism to teaching? First and foremost, they must create a campus climate that supports and rewards effective teaching and accord such teaching a status equal to that of scholarly research and publication. This turnabout can take place only at the initiative and with the guidance of the institution's administrative leaders. Only they can use the power of office to champion teaching and publicly crusade for recognition of its importance. They can, for example, set up or join forums to inform academia of the calculable value of effective teaching, and they can actively promote institutional policies and practices that recognize and reward effective teaching. In short, administrative leaders can play a decisive role in determining how much importance their institutions place on teaching and its improvement.

How Administrators Can Improve Teaching offers college and university administrators the kind of ready-to-use and research-based information required in order to provide leadership and support to foster really effective teaching at their institutions. This book is not simply another clarion call to action; instead, it is a hard-hitting critique of the current administrative climate for teaching and a well-grounded guide for achieving needed, and overdue, changes in campus culture, teacher training programs, evaluation and development of teaching performance, and faculty rewards and incentives. Overall, the contributors reaffirm the pivotal role of classroom teaching in the academic profession.

Earlier books on improving teaching effectiveness have

mainly been collections of instructional techniques, often focused on a specific academic discipline, that overlook the role of administrators. In fact, the success of individual faculty efforts as well as those of faculty development specialists in improving teaching will probably be sporadic until such efforts are fully supported and encouraged at key administrative levels.

How Administrators Can Improve Teaching focuses directly on the special role administrators play in fostering high-quality teaching. The chapter authors specify the strategies and programs administrators can use to effect changes needed to achieve teaching excellence. This book does more than challenge the status quo. It spells out in specific terms the kinds of leadership and support that must be in place to ensure effective teaching.

Audience of the Book

The book is written for presidents, provosts, academic vice-presidents, deans, and department chairs, who are the essential partners in working to provide administrative leadership for teaching effectiveness. The practical suggestions and recommendations presented should prove of value to these administrators, whether they are in private or public institutions. Graduate students in higher education, especially those planning careers in academic administration, should also find the book stimulating and helpful.

The book distills not only the literature but also, and more important, the personal experience of each contributor. The contributors are nationally prominent educators who have done seminal work in the improvement of college and university teaching. Collectively, their names read like the membership roster in a teaching-and-learning hall of fame. In addition to being experts in their fields, almost all contributors have held teaching as well as administrative positions and consequently are eminently qualified to write on their chosen subjects.

Overview of the Contents

The first part of the book examines the college and university climate in which teaching takes place and the way that climate affects the faculty.

In Chapter One, Seldin discusses how and why many administrators fail to encourage the kind of organizational and academic environment needed for effective teaching—and how to change the campus climate to make it more responsive to effective teaching. Also discussed is the teaching portfolio, which is a new method for documenting teaching effectiveness.

In Chapter Two, Rice and Austin examine organizational factors that favor high faculty morale and motivation to teach, such as participatory leadership, organizational momentum, and faculty development programs. They also discuss an array of formal and informal ways in which deans and department chairs can demonstrate their commitment to teaching.

The second part of the book focuses on specific strategies for improvement and addresses the key changes needed to support and reward teaching and to accord it a status equal to that of scholarly research and publication.

In Chapter Three, Green examines the changing world of higher education and stresses the need for a new kind of administrative leadership. She discusses the importance of institutional culture as a dynamic partner in leadership and offers recommendations to administrators who want to elevate the status of teaching but whose administrative practices send a different message.

In Chapter Four, Lucas points out the department chair's pivotal role as change agent in creating a campus climate in which teaching is valued and rewarded. She presents many practical interventions for creating such a climate and discusses many significant aspects of teaching, learning, and motivating students.

In Chapter Five, Cashin explores successful approaches in assessing teaching performance. Drawing on the research literature and his own practical experience, he explains what really works and what does not work and makes recommendations for using student ratings, course materials, classroom observations, and audio- and videotapes.

In Chapter Six, Menges describes how to use evaluation information to improve teaching. He delineates the administrator's role in creating a campus climate conducive to effective teaching and presents ways to assist faculty members in self-improvement activities. Menges presents many practical examples of self-improvement activities, based on an innovative four-component model of the teaching-learning process.

In Chapter Seven, Cross considers classroom research as a vehicle for improving teaching and learning, examining the changing relationship between classroom research and faculty development. She offers concrete examples of classroom research projects, differentiates them from traditional educational research, and describes what administrators can do to encourage classroom research at their institutions.

In Chapter Eight, Chickering and Potter investigate the tight bond between public institutions and state government. They argue that understanding the powerful role of the state and knowing how best to work with it are critical if leadership and resources to improve teaching are to be maintained. They offer practical strategies for administrators.

Part Three presents real-world examples of what is needed to reaffirm the crucial role of teaching in the academic profession and includes a chapter-by-chapter summary and key recommendations for academic leaders.

In Chapter Nine, Sheridan examines the key role administrators can play in placing excellence in teaching on an equal plane with excellence in scholarship. She discusses how administrators can strengthen the perception of the importance of teaching by making it more visible to the community and why the preparation of graduate teaching assistants and the initiation of new faculty should include demonstrations of student learning differences.

In Chapter Ten, McCabe and Jenrette discuss how Miami-Dade Community College is making effective teaching an institutional priority. Step by step, they present what has worked and what has not worked in Miami-Dade's experience and offer guidelines and strategies that can benefit administrators at other institutions.

In Chapter Eleven, Seldin summarizes key recommendations for actions administrators can take to bring about the needed changes to encourage teaching excellence throughout the institution.

Croton-on-Hudson, New York   Peter Seldin
July 1990

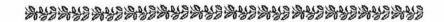

The Authors

Peter Seldin is professor of management at Pace University, Pleasantville, New York. He received his B.A. degree (1963) in psychology from Hobart and William Smith Colleges, his M.B.A. degree (1966) in management from Long Island University, and his Ph.D. degree (1974) in education from Fordham University. He completed his postdoctoral work in evaluation and development at the University of London in 1976.

Seldin has designed and conducted seminars for faculty and administrators in colleges and universities throughout the United States and in Japan, England, Canada, Mexico, Egypt, Switzerland, Israel, and Africa. He is a frequent speaker at national and international conferences and has served on the core committee of the Professional and Organizational Development Network, on the program advisory committee for the International Conference on Improving University Teaching, and in the National Leadership Group of the American Council on Education.

His books include *How Colleges Evaluate Professors* (1975), *Teaching Professors to Teach* (1977), *Successful Faculty Evaluation Programs* (1980), *Changing Practices in Faculty Evaluation* (1984), and *Evaluating and Developing Administrative Performance* (1988), and he is editor of a quarterly sourcebook in the Jossey-Bass New Directions for Teaching and Learning Series (*Coping with Faculty Stress* [1987]). He has contributed numerous articles on the teaching profession, evaluating and developing performance, and academic culture to such publications as the *New York Times* and *Change* magazine.

Ann E. Austin is research assistant professor in the Department of Educational Leadership in the George Peabody College at Vanderbilt University. She received her B.A. degree (1976) in history from Bates College, her M.S. degree (1978) in higher and postsecondary education from Syracuse University, her M.A. degree (1982) in American culture from the University of Michigan, and her Ph.D. degree (1984) in higher education from the University of Michigan. Austin has been on the faculty at Oklahoma State University, has coauthored *The Academic Workplace: New Demands, Heightened Tensions* (1983), and has been one of the principal researchers, with R. Eugene Rice, for the Council of Independent Colleges' project on the academic workplace in liberal arts colleges.

William E. Cashin is director of the Center for Faculty Evaluation and Development at Kansas State University. The center provides services to other colleges and universities, using the IDEA system—Kansas State's student rating form— and seminars and consultation on evaluating faculty and improving teaching. Cashin received his Ph.D. degree (1969) in counseling psychology from Catholic University, Washington, D.C. Cashin is on the editorial boards of *Teaching of Psychology* and the *Journal of Educational Psychology*. In 1987 he gave one of the American Psychological Association's G. Stanley Hall lectures entitled "Using Evaluation Data to Improve College Classroom Teaching."

Arthur W. Chickering is University Professor at George Mason University. From 1977 to 1988 he was Distinguished Professor and director of the Center for the Study of Higher Education at Memphis State University. From 1970 to 1977 he served as the founding vice-president for academic affairs at

Empire State College. He received his B.A. degree (1950) in modern comparative literature from Wesleyan University, his M.A. degree (1951) in teaching English from the Graduate School of Education, Harvard University, and his Ph.D. degree (1959) in school psychology from Teachers College, Columbia University.

K. Patricia Cross is Elizabeth and Edward Connor Professor of Higher Education at the University of California, Berkeley. She received her B.S. degree (1948) in mathematics from Illinois State University, her A.M. degree (1951) in psychology from the University of Illinois, and her Ph.D. degree (1958) in social psychology from the University of Illinois. Cross has served as professor, researcher, or administrator at the University of Illinois, Cornell University, the Educational Testing Service, University of Nebraska, and the Harvard Graduate School of Education. Her writing and research are most often about nontraditional college students, community colleges, and teaching and learning.

Madeleine F. Green has been vice-president of the American Council on Education (ACE) since June 1987. She has served as director of the Center for Leadership Development at ACE since August 1982 and as director of the ACE Fellows Program since 1978. She received her B.A. degree (1967) in French literature from Radcliffe College, and M.A. (1969) and Ph.D. (1973) degrees in French literature from Columbia University. Her most recent book is *Leaders for a New Era: Strategies for Higher Education* (1988).

Mardee S. Jenrette is an associate professor of biology at Miami-Dade Community College and currently directs the Teaching/Learning Project in addition to teaching full time. She is a past chair of staff and program development at Miami-Dade Community College. She received her B.S. degree (1963) in zoology from Cornell University and her M.S. degree (1965) in marine biology from the University of Hawaii.

Ann F. Lucas is professor and campus chair of the Department of Management at Fairleigh Dickinson University, where she is also founder and former director of the Office of Professional and Organizational Development, and former chair of the Psychology Department. A licensed psychologist, with a diploma in clinical psychology, she received her B.S. degree in psychology from Seton Hall University and her M.A. and Ph.D. degrees in psychology from Fordham University. She is editor of *The Department Chairperson's Role in Enhancing College Teaching* (1989), a Jossey-Bass quarterly in the New Directions for Teaching and Learning series.

Robert H. McCabe is president of Miami-Dade Community College and is also chairman of the College Board, board member of the Council for Aid to Education, and a member of the Association of Governing Boards of Universities and Colleges. He received his B.Ed. degree (1952) in history from the University of Miami, his M.A. degree (1959) in educational administration from Appalachian State College, and his Ph.D. degree (1963) in business administration from the University of Texas, Austin.

Robert J. Menges is professor of education and social policy at Northwestern University and program director at Northwestern's Center for the Teaching Professions. He received his B.A. (1960) degree from Gettysburg College, his M.A. degree (1963) from Boston University, and his Ed.D. degree (1967) from Columbia University Teachers College. He is author of *Key Resources on Teaching, Learning, Curriculum, and Faculty Development* (1988, with B. C. Mathis).

David L. Potter is vice-president for executive affairs at George Mason University and has served as assistant director for academic affairs at the State Council of Higher Education for Virginia. He received his B.A. degree (1964) in history from Amherst College, and his M.A. (1971) and Ph.D. (1972) degrees in social science from the Maxwell School of Citizenship and Public Affairs, Syracuse University.

R. Eugene Rice is vice-president and dean of faculty at Antioch College and was formerly senior fellow at the Carnegie Foundation for the Advancement of Teaching, Princeton, where he wrote a special report with Ernest Boyer entitled "The New American Scholar: Toward a Broader Conception of Scholarship." Rice received his B.A. degree (1957) in philosophy from Pasadena College, his S.T.B. degree (1960) in social ethics from Harvard Divinity School, and his Ph.D. degree (1970) in religion and sociology from Harvard University.

Harriet W. Sheridan is professor of English and director of the Center for the Advancement of College Teaching at Brown University. She received her B.A. degree (1944) in English from Hunter College, her M.A. degree (1945) in medieval English literature from Smith College, and her Ph.D. degree (1950) in medieval English literature from Yale University. She has served as dean and acting president at Carleton College and as dean at Brown University (1979 through 1986).

How Administrators
Can Improve Teaching

PART ONE

Key Influences on
Teaching Quality

CHAPTER 1

❧❧❧❧❧❧❧❧❧❧❧❧❧❧❧

Academic Environments and Teaching Effectiveness
Peter Seldin

The vast majority of colleges and universities claim to be strongly committed to effective teaching. College brochures and catalogues proclaim dedication to high-quality instruction, insisting that although the faculty may be scholarly, true focus of the institution is on teaching.

Many who teach in today's colleges and universities would challenge this portrayal, noting that their personal experience belies this official reverence for quality teaching. For example, it is not uncommon for an academic administrator to emphasize to visiting parents and students the institution's commitment to teaching while luring a renowned professor to the institution by promising little or no teaching. Despite rhetoric to the contrary, it is clearly a trend that colleges and universities give more consideration to research and scholarly performance than to teaching in their recruitment, promotion, and tenure decisions. Even the forms completed by faculty seeking promotion reflect this emphasis; rarely is even one-sixth of the space on these forms devoted to the applicant's teaching contributions.

Teaching as an Undervalued Profession

It is a fact of academic life that teaching is widely undervalued today. The approach seems to be to talk about the

3

importance of teaching but to evaluate faculty primarily on the basis of scholarly achievements and professional activities. Anyone who doubts this should observe a faculty recruitment or promotion committee meeting and note how little attention is given to the candidate's teaching performance.

The faculty member more interested in teaching than in scholarly research is soon forced by the institution's reward system to "go with the program." At a recent conference, one professor offered this typical comment: "Theoretically, teaching is still important at my college. But in practice, my salary and promotion are determined by scholarship. That's why I channel my energy into research and put my teaching on the back burner." A similar view was voiced by another professor: "I can write a conference paper in the time it would take me to revise my teaching notes. I'll get to the notes eventually. But for now, I'll write the paper. I have to think of my career."

To illustrate the dominating role of research and scholarship, Astin (1985, p. 184) describes an event honoring a university president:

> Not a single [speaker] said anything about the educational [teaching] effectiveness . . . of the institution. All the comments were directed toward the institution's effectiveness in conducting research. . . . A visiting Martian would have concluded that the university . . . was a research institute rather than an educational institution.

Why Does Teaching Have Second-Rate Status? Elmore (1989) suggests that one answer to this question lies in the values, norms, and reward structure of academic institutions. Currently, the real work of the institution (to which is attached real status) is the production and diffusion of new knowledge. Only a few institutions, Elmore points out, have been willing and able to sustain a long-term commitment to serious analysis and critical discourse about teaching.

Astin (1985) is persuaded that the low value assigned to teaching is because the products of good research and scholarship are more visible and quantifiable than those of good teaching. As a result, the institution enhances its prestige more readily by recruiting outstanding scholars than by recruiting outstanding teachers. Also, outstanding scholars are much better "magnets" for attracting more funding and brighter students.

Seldin (1989) agrees, noting that when teaching is pitted against research, teaching automatically loses. Teaching, he says, is largely a private affair that goes on between professor and students behind a closed classroom door. The results of research are published and become a matter of public discussion. It is not surprising that colleges and universities set a greater store by research and fail to reward even outstanding teaching performance. An institution that does otherwise goes against the tide.

Thus, in many institutions an excellent teacher comes second compared to a mediocre teacher with flashy research accomplishments. The very basis of the institutional reward system is the belief that working with, contributing to, and pursuing knowledge is superior to teaching (see Sheridan, this volume). In fact, Astin (1985, p. 187) argues that the faculty job description, which typically highlights teaching, research and scholarship, and service, is a "fantasy and a smoke screen." The reality is that the institution rewards only scholarly activity and gives lip service to the other faculty accomplishments.

There are still other reasons why teaching is subject to benign neglect. One is a notable lack of teaching preparation during graduate education. Edgerton (1988, p. 7) comments:

> Our faculty come to us strong in content and blissfully ignorant of anything having to do with theories of learning or strategies of teaching rooted in pedagogical content knowledge. In their knowledge of their discipline, as the saying goes, they stand on the shoulders of giants. In their knowledge of teaching, they stand on the ground.

True, some institutions, such as Syracuse University, are turning their attention to training doctoral students to teach, but these are the exception. In general, graduate education continues to focus almost exclusively on knowledge of the discipline.

In some institutions, the reason that teaching is relegated to lesser status is the vocal insistence by some academics that teaching performance does not lend itself to evaluation. Good teaching, they insist, defies definition; it is so singular an art that it is incapable of measurement. Confronted by the need to evaluate their colleagues' teaching, remarks Elmore (1989, p. 12), they resort to such rhetoric as the professor "doesn't seem to be getting through to the students" or the professor "knows the subject but doesn't seem to be able to get it across."

In truth, however, teaching can be assessed as rigorously as research and publication and has been for years by many institutions (see Cashin and also Menges, this volume). As Seldin (1984, p. 124) points out, "Student ratings, classroom visits, colleague reviews of teaching materials, alumni opinions, self-assessments, and special incidents have been systematically gathered and judiciously interpreted at many institutions." Such researchers and writers as Eble (1972); Braskamp, Brandenburg, and Ory (1984); Lowman (1984); Licata (1986); Sorcinelli (1986); Miller (1987); and McKeachie (personal communication, June 1989) hold the same view.

Has teaching always had second-rank status? The answer is no. The origin of research and publication in academic life can be traced to the universities of nineteenth-century Prussia. The tradition became firmly established in American colleges and universities in the years immediately preceding the First World War. At that time, there was no conflict between teaching and research and scholarly activity. Nisbet (1967, p. 22) concludes that the absence of conflict was because the kind of research going on in colleges and universities was "small in scope, personal in character, finite in aspiration, and on the whole, optional." Research and scholarly activity were simply considered an adjunct to teaching.

Today it is a very different story. Institutions across the country have turned to faculty research and publication, rather than outstanding teaching, as their means to institutional distinction. Edgerton (1989, p. 15) finds that "regional universities have been tightening the screws on faculty to publish. Some highly selective liberal arts colleges are beginning to refer to themselves as 'research colleges.'"

What makes the situation even worse, reports Cross (1986), is that many faculty members engage in research and publish articles not because they have anything important to say but because they need publications for their vitae. New journals are launched, she says, not to disseminate knowledge but to provide outlets for upwardly striving faculty members.

In speaking about the increasing emphasis on research and publication, one professor lamented, half in jest, "At the rate things are going, it would not be surprising someday to hear some undergraduates rating their teachers not on their classroom skills but rather on their record of scholarly activity. The day may not be too far off when a student will say, 'Take Smith's course; she just got a $750,000 grant from the National Science Foundation.'"

Does Today's Campus Climate Support Efforts to Improve Teaching? The answer is clearly no. This may be why so few faculty members participate in programs offered by faculty development centers to improve teaching performance. Some professors do not participate because of inertia; others, because they are fearful of publicly displaying their teaching techniques. Many stay away because they know that promotion and tenure decisions depend primarily on research and scholarly performance.

This view is given voice by many professors. For example, at a recent dinner meeting, one professor remarked, "What are the things that count? Research, publications, grants. I come up for tenure next year. Why should I spend time trying to improve my teaching?" Another professor commented, "We have a teaching improvement center at my college. Why should I go? They don't reward you for teaching."

A third said bluntly, "I'd like to be a better teacher. But I will perish if I don't publish."

Many colleges and universities say the right thing about the importance of teaching and some even establish teaching improvement centers. But too often these centers are merely window dressing. These centers are often understaffed and underbudgeted, and because the faculty sense the institution's priorities, attendance is often sparse.

The problem is not that faculty are uninterested in teaching. On the contrary, the Carnegie Foundation for the Advancement of Teaching reports that 72 percent of all professors say that their primary interest is in teaching rather than research. But 59 percent of professors report that it is difficult to receive tenure without publishing scholarly work. In an interview published in the *Chronicle of Higher Education,* Ernest Boyer, the Carnegie Foundation's president, notes that a comparison of these results with those of a previous survey indicates that although more professors report an interest in teaching, more also report that it is difficult to achieve tenure without publishing. This suggests to Boyer that institutional practice and faculty preference are moving in different directions (Mooney, 1989).

Changing the Campus Climate to Foster Effective Teaching

To bring a new professionalism to teaching requires action and a campus climate that supports and rewards effective teaching, placing it on an equal status level with scholarly research and publication.

Perhaps the place to start is by recognizing that excellent teaching demands scholarly expertise equally as great as but of a different order than research and publication. As Seldin (1984, p. 124) points out, "The same high level of conceptual and analytical thinking, the same time, energy, and personal dedication that characterize superior research and publication also characterize superior teaching." Because of special interest, temperament, or inclination, some faculty members favor one or the other, but this is often a matter of degree rather than exclusion and may shift from time to time.

On this point, Eble (1972, p. 28) states, "A minimum reward system should lead faculty members to pursue knowledge and to profess it, to devote their energies to one at some periods and to the other at other times. The system should give all members of the faculty the opportunity and incentive to develop both as teachers and as men and women of knowledge." The road to promotion and tenure should be as easily traveled by superior teachers as by superior scholars. There is a genuine and pressing need for both in higher education (Seldin, 1989).

If colleges and universities are going to embrace superior teachers and superior scholars equally, providing the initiative and the guidance for such transformation falls to administrative leaders (see Lucas, this volume). They must champion the importance of teaching and personally crusade for this idea. In a sense, they must stake their careers on this point and actively seek and find forums from which to broadcast to academia the importance of teaching. To support their verbal endorsement, they must introduce and promote appropriate institutional policies and practices.

What kinds of concrete action might be taken to support a higher priority for teaching? Experience suggests that the following five approaches, used in combination, work well:

1. Changing the campus environment to make it more responsive to teaching
2. Providing the proper setting and tools to support instruction
3. Assisting graduate students to develop their teaching skills
4. Using appropriate rewards to improve teaching
5. Establishing an effective faculty development system.

Changing the Campus Environment to Make It More Responsive to Teaching. Colleges and universities must provide the means to breathe new life into teaching. Each professor must be encouraged to set his or her own professional goals and style in the classroom. Experimentation in the classroom should be a normal part of professional growth and practice. Teaching loads should be kept to reasonable limits so the professor can keep abreast of changes in the discipline. A good environment for teaching also nurtures collegial dialogue in which peer review of teaching is as common as peer review of research. It is an environment in which, as Edgerton (1988, p. 8) suggests, "Professors ask their colleagues for comment on the syllabus of a course as routinely as they ask for comment on the prospectus for a book."

Harvard University president Derek Bok (1986) cautions that building an environment that encourages and rewards good teaching does not magically evolve from one dramatic initiative but requires a painstaking administrative undertaking the final goal of which is to place teaching and scholarship on an equal footing.

What might such an administrative undertaking be? Seldin (1989) suggests it might include the following:

1. Serious attention would be paid both to superior teachers and superior researchers when deciding whom to appoint, whom to promote, and to whom to give tenure. Teaching quality would also be important in determining salary increases.
2. The definition of scholarship would be broadened beyond the discovery of new knowledge and would involve the integration of new and existing knowledge. This body of knowledge would be applied to problems and transmitted to students.
3. Desirable faculty members would no longer be lured to the institution by promises of low or no teaching loads.
4. Faculty members would find ways to use their research activities as a tool to enhance the teaching-learning process and would be questioned on this point during the annual updating of their faculty activities.
5. Professors would be kept current on the general developments in higher education, especially developments

directly related to teaching and learning. Particularly important would be techniques for assessing the effects of teaching on student learning.

6. The instructional program would be subject to periodic reviews and proposals for its improvement, which would help eliminate obsolete programs, revitalize old programs, and provide a basis for developing new programs.

7. Careful, systematic student evaluation of courses would help professors discover areas in which their teaching and course materials needed improvement. Student feedback would help professors learn to enhance their teaching skills and strategies.

8. A comprehensive program would assist in the personal and professional development of faculty members. The program would include written materials, colloquia, seminars, a videotape of the professor teaching a class, and a discussion of teaching strengths and weaknesses with the aid of an experienced and supportive instructional improvement specialist.

Providing the Proper Setting and Tools to Support Instruction. Although the size, shape, and furnishing of rooms do subtly influence learning, superior teachers probably can overcome the negative effects of physical setting. Nonetheless, suitable teaching settings make a difference for teachers and learners and are not particularly expensive to provide. Even such simple conveniences as hooks on which to hang coats can make a difference.

Despite the wonders of indirect lighting and climate control, the amounts of light, air, heat, and noise in the classroom are often not better controlled than they were in less technologically advanced times. Unfortunately, classroom conditions in too many colleges and universities are a poor advertisement for the institution's concerns with teaching. In the ironic words of one professor, "It's easier to get a $5,000 piece of machinery here than it is to get a supply of chalk and erasers." Administrators need to know when floors do not get swept, when equipment does not work, and when classroom

supplies have run out. Failure to pay attention to these details
indicates to professors that teaching is considered second class
by the institution.

Similarly, faculty offices that are cramped and unat-
tractive, with no room for books and files and lacking in
privacy for discussions with students, or a secretarial pool
that is inadequate to handle the paperwork required of
teachers also indicates the institution's disinterest in teaching.

This is not to imply that teaching conditions should be
luxurious. The point is that if faculty morale is to be boosted
and teaching held in high esteem, institutions should pay
serious attention to and correct environmental shortcomings.
Administrators can underscore the importance of teaching by
restructuring their institution's annual budget to allocate sufficient money for the institution's "teaching plant," as it does
for its physical plant. Moreover, long-term teaching needs
should be regularly addressed to sustain the institution's new
respect for teaching.

***Assisting Graduate Students to Develop Their Teaching
Skills.*** What does graduate education contribute to the development of faculty as teachers? Sadly, at present, it is very
little. Most doctoral programs aim primarily at preparing
graduate students to be research specialists within their particular disciplines.

As a recent report of the Association of American Colleges (1985, p. 29) concluded, "The emphasis of the graduate
school years is almost exclusively on the development of substantive knowledge and research skills. Any introduction to
teaching comes only incidentally. . . . The [doctoral degree]
candidate is rarely, if ever, introduced to any of the ingredients
that make up the art, the science, and the special responsibilities of teaching."

Considering this situation, it is not surprising that
most new faculty members enter the classroom untrained and
ill prepared to teach. Some may serve as teaching assistants
(TAs), but not because the experience is useful in their development as classroom teachers. The reason they become TAs,

says Eble (1988, p. 201), is that "it supports graduate students financially and provides a source of cheap instruction in the undergraduate college."

How can graduate students receive additional training in their careers as teachers? A blue-ribbon panel of the Higher Education Research Program suggests a teaching apprenticeship within graduate education programs. Practice teaching, close supervision, and feedback, when made part of the apprenticeship, says the panel, will help the doctoral student learn how to be effective in the classroom. A key aspect underlying the program is the clear understanding that graduate professors will be held accountable for the quality of the teachers they turn out (Watkins, 1989). If graduate school professors are held accountable for the quality of research *and* the quality of teaching of their graduate students, one can reasonably assume they will work hard to make their students competent as teachers and as researchers.

Using Appropriate Rewards to Improve Teaching. Over the past decade, I have visited more than one hundred college and university campuses. One purpose of those visits was to discuss, in depth, college teaching, especially teaching on the undergraduate level. In the course of these visits, it was most frequently suggested that the best route to improve teaching was to change the reward system. The most frequent criticism of the reward system was that teaching was pitted against research, to teaching's detriment. Institutions are clearly biased on the side of research and fail to reward even outstanding teachers.

There is some evidence to support the above view. Tuckman (1979) studied the academic reward system, surveying professors in twenty-two disciplines from public and private institutions. He found that research and publication were rewarded in most disciplines. In contrast, he found that public service was rewarded in ten fields and that outstanding teaching (identified by the receipt of recognition for teaching excellence) was rewarded in only two of the twenty-two disciplines.

Clearly, the reward system needs to be reworked so that, as the Higher Education Research Program panel suggests, there is greater recognition of superior teaching. Watkins (1989) reports that the panel urged colleges and universities to make teaching of central importance in hiring, promotion, and tenure decisions. It does little good, according to the panel, to espouse teaching excellence if faculty consistently perceive that only research is considered important.

A productive way to encourage outstanding teaching is for administrators to provide meaningful rewards to faculty. This presupposes an answer to an earlier question: How can professors document their classroom performance or their outstanding efforts to improve that performance? One means of providing such documentation, an approach increasingly recognized and respected, is the teaching portfolio.

What is a teaching portfolio? It is a bringing together of a professor's most important teaching strengths and accomplishments. It houses in one place the scope and quality of a professor's teaching performance. The portfolio is to teaching what lists of publications, grants, and honors are to research and scholarship. It can be used to provide specific data about teaching effectiveness to those who judge performance or as a springboard for self-improvement. The purpose for which the portfolio is to be used determines what is included and how it is presented.

The material found in a teaching portfolio includes, among other possible items, the following:

1. A list of every course taught, including enrollments, grade distributions, and a brief description of the way the course was taught
2. Representative course syllabi that detail course content and objectives, teaching methods, readings, homework assignments, and a reflective statement as to why the class was so constructed
3. A description of steps taken to evaluate and improve one's teaching, including changes resulting from self-evaluation, time spent reading journals on improving

teaching, attempts to implement new ideas, or participation in seminars and workshops on improving teaching

4. Student evaluation data suggesting improvements or producing an overall rating of effectiveness or satisfaction
5. Student scores on professor-made or standardized tests, as evidence of student learning
6. Student essays, field-work reports, or laboratory workbooks
7. A record of students who succeed in advanced courses of study in the field
8. Statements from colleagues who have observed the professor in the classroom as members of a teaching team or independent observers
9. Statements from colleagues who have systematically reviewed the professor's classroom materials, the course syllabi, course assignments, and testing and grading practices
10. Record of participation in local, regional, state, or national activities relating to the teaching of courses in the professor's discipline
11. Statements by alumni on the quality of instruction
12. Records of student success in graduate school
13. Evidence of self-evaluation by the professor, including a personal assessment of teaching-related activities
14. Contributions to professional journals on teaching in the professor's discipline
15. A videotape of the professor teaching a typical class.

The teaching portfolio concept is being successfully used today. Among the institutions operating a portfolio program, or at least an adaptation of it, are Gordon College (Massachusetts), Indiana University–Bloomington, Miami-Dade Community College (Florida), and the University of West Florida. Other institutions are field testing the portfolio concept.

One thing is clear: When teaching portfolios are used, the reward system is more responsive to teaching. The reason is probably that portfolios provide the much-needed information and evidence about teaching performance that helps promotion and tenure review committees accord the teaching function its proper value.

Establishing an Effective Faculty Development System.
There have been many attempts to broaden faculty competence, but most have focused almost exclusively on helping professors master subject matter. Sabbatical leaves, trips to meetings of professional societies, and research grants reflect this kind of effort. Scant attention has been given to how professors can better impart their knowledge to their students. Eble and McKeachie (1985) and Seldin (1989) acknowledge that the thrust of faculty development activities during the 1970s was to develop faculty members as teachers, but—on a national basis—such activities have diminished and are less well supported today.

However, at a number of colleges and universities, faculty development centers and offices with strong emphasis on teaching are alive and well and are found at such public and private institutions as Ball State University (Indiana), Colorado State University, Delaware State College, Henderson Community College (Kentucky), Kennesaw College (Georgia), Miami University (Ohio), the University of Georgia, the University of Tennessee, and the University of Texas.

The academic administrators of these and other institutions recognize the need for faculty members to gain theoretical and practical training as effective teachers. In the process, they question and reconsider their past precepts of teaching and learning.

The nature of faculty development programs varies from one campus to another owing to differences in history, mission, faculty interests, internal politics, and staff expertise. But four main approaches to faculty development programs that stress teaching improvement are identifiable:

1. In-service workshops that develop specific skills
2. Feedback that provides professors with information on

students' and colleagues' perceptions of their teaching effectiveness

3. Lectures and discussion groups devoted to broad issues of higher education
4. Financial incentives that encourage innovative instructional practices.

The key characteristics of faculty development programs that aim at improving teachers and teaching needs are identified by Seldin (1989). These programs are

1. Tailored to the institution's culture.
2. Structured along multiple-approach lines to meet individual preferences, schedules, and styles.
3. Supported clearly and visibly by top-level administrators.
4. Aided in their design and management by a faculty advisory group.
5. Started small, perhaps as a pilot project targeting specific needs or groups.
6. Funded by a specific percentage of an institution's general operating fund.
7. Publicizing their programs throughout the year.
8. Kept apart from the institution's promotion and tenure decision making.
9. A central source for gathering, selecting, and disseminating information about teaching and learning to the faculty.
10. Building a climate of trust, openness, mutual respect, and interdependence.
11. Led by directors who offer strong leadership on campus and work effectively with institutional governing groups.
12. Located on campuses where outstanding teaching is recognized and rewarded.
13. Holding to the bedrock belief that faculty members merit, rather than need, help.

In an important way, faculty development is linked with evaluation of teaching. Student ratings, self-assessment, videotaped classroom performance, and peer observation combine to offer professors a view of themselves as others perceive them (see Cashin, this volume). Does the use of evaluation automatically result in improved teaching? For most professors, probably not. Ratings are more likely to produce a salutary effect when discussed with the professor by a sympathetic and knowledgeable teaching improvement specialist, who can offer appropriate counsel on how to make improvements.

Wilson (1987) reports that the University of California at Berkeley has developed an interesting fusion of student evaluation and faculty development. Called Personal Improvement Teaching Guides, this approach is tailored to the needs of individual faculty members. A twenty-four-item student evaluation form is used as a starting point, and the guides include very specific descriptions of successful teaching practices, matched to the instructor's lowest-rated items. Thus, faculty members are supplied with simple, proven, practical suggestions that can be used immediately to improve their teaching.

A Sampling of Institutions
That Take Teaching Seriously

The idea of taking teaching seriously has gone well beyond theory. Today, many institutions—public and private, large and small—are nurturing and rewarding effective teaching. A sampling of these institutions follows:

- Miami-Dade Community College (Florida) will soon require all new professors to take two more graduate courses, one on teaching and learning and the other on techniques to assess teaching effects on student learning. Established professors will be encouraged and rewarded to take both courses. (See McCabe and Jenrette, this volume, for a complete description of the Miami-Dade program.)
- At Haverford College (Pennsylvania), senior administrators conduct exit interviews with graduating seniors and

ask questions such as "Did the teaching at Haverford live up to your expectations?"

- The University of Georgia has established a Senior Teaching Fellows Program that enables fellows to meet regularly to discuss issues and concerns related to undergraduate teaching. Each of the eight fellows, selected annually, receives a grant of up to $4,000 for an individual project to improve a particular undergraduate course or course sequence. (See Green, this volume, for a more complete description of the University of Georgia program.)

- At the University of Redlands (California), a course designed for first-year students was developed and taught by the university's president, vice-president for academic affairs, dean, and chaplain.

- At Pace University (New York), the academic dean of the School of Business adopted a formal weighting system for appraising faculty performance in which teaching and scholarly research were given equal weight.

- At Alverno College (Wisconsin), teaching outweighs research in the professor's hierarchy of responsibilities. The college is now considered a "teach-well-or-perish" institution rather than a "publish-or-perish" institution.

- Ball State University (Indiana) has developed a Partners in Teaching Improvement Project in which selected faculty members team with a partner to observe each other's classes; each week they meet to discuss their observations and suggestions for each other's teaching improvement.

- Trenton State College (New Jersey) has developed a five-pronged approach that includes: (1) funding for faculty engaged in professional development activities, (2) new faculty mentoring, (3) a Center for Instructional Enhancement that plans and schedules faculty workshops and discussions, (4) departmental curriculum development, and (5) an award for distinguished research.

- The University of Denver Business School has developed an Instructional Management System that revolves around a new student evaluation program, which in turn helps faculty better understand how students perceive teaching efforts and helps identify teaching areas that need improvement. The system includes instructional seminars wherein such topics as behavioral theory, presentation skills, case teaching, and audiovisual techniques are discussed.

(Rice and Austin, this volume, offer other examples of institutions that are demonstrating a firm commitment to teaching.)

Conclusion

On many college and university campuses today, the institutional bias toward research and scholarship tends to discourage teaching effectiveness. A few colleges and universities go against the tide by considering outstanding teachers to be the equal of outstanding researchers. It is time for more colleges to follow this course. In the succeeding chapters in this book, administrators can find pragmatic advice on how to nurture good teaching and on how to close the "credibility gap" between talking about good teaching and actively supporting it.

What is needed is to (1) change the campus environment, (2) provide the proper setting and tools, (3) assist graduate students to develop their teaching skills, (4) use appropriate rewards, and (5) establish an effective faculty development system.

Administrators cannot transform today's inhospitable climate for teaching simply by offering prizes for outstanding teaching. Teaching will attain real value only when institutions recruit, promote, and tenure outstanding teachers.

Arrowsmith (1967, p. 58) notes that today colleges and universities "are as uncongenial to teaching as the Mojave Desert to a clutch of Druid priests. If you want to restore a Druid priesthood, you cannot do it by offering prizes for Druid-of-the-year. If you want Druids, you must grow forests."

References

Arrowsmith, W. "The Future of Teaching." In C.B.T. Lee (ed.), *Improving College Teaching*. Washington, D.C.: American Council on Education, 1967.

Association of American Colleges. *Integrity in the College Curriculum: A Report to the Academic Community*. Washington, D.C.: Association of American Colleges, 1985.

Astin, A. W. *Achieving Educational Excellence*. San Francisco: Jossey-Bass, 1985.

Bok, D. *Higher Learning*. Cambridge, Mass.: Harvard University Press, 1986.

Braskamp, L. A., Brandenburg, D. C., and Ory, J. C. *Evaluating Teaching Effectiveness: A Practical Guide*. Newbury Park, Calif.: Sage, 1984.

Cross, K. P. "Taking Teaching Seriously." Paper presented at the AAHE National Conference on Higher Education, Washington, D.C., 1986.

Eble, K. E. *Professors as Teachers*. San Francisco: Jossey-Bass, 1972.

Eble, K. E. *The Craft of Teaching*. (2nd ed.) San Francisco: Jossey-Bass, 1988.

Eble, K. E., and McKeachie, W. J. *Improving Undergraduate Education Through Faculty Development*. San Francisco: Jossey-Bass, 1985.

Edgerton, R. "All Roads Lead to Teaching." *AAHE Bulletin*, Apr. 1988, pp. 3–9.

Edgerton, R. "Report from the President." *AAHE Bulletin*, June 1989, pp. 14–17.

Elmore, R. F. "How We Teach Is What We Teach." *AAHE Bulletin*, Apr. 1989, pp. 11–14.

Licata, C. M. *Post-Tenure Faculty Evaluation: Threat or Opportunity*. ASHE-ERIC Higher Education Report no. 1. Washington, D.C.: Association for the Study of Higher Education, 1986.

Lowman, J. *Mastering the Techniques of Teaching*. San Francisco: Jossey-Bass, 1984.

Miller, R. I. *Evaluating Faculty for Promotion and Tenure.* San Francisco: Jossey-Bass, 1987.

Mooney, C. J. "Three in Four Professors Think Their Undergraduate Students Are Seriously Underprepared, Carnegie Study Finds." *Chronicle of Higher Education,* Apr. 16, 1989, p. A13.

Nisbet, R. A. "Conflicting Academic Loyalties." In C.B.T. Lee (ed.), *Improving College Teaching.* Washington, D.C.: American Council on Education, 1967.

Seldin, P. *Changing Practices in Faculty Evaluation.* San Francisco: Jossey-Bass, 1984.

Seldin, P. "Academic Culture." Paper presented at the Workshop on Evaluating Faculty and Institutional Performance, Universidad de Monterrey, Mexico, May 1989.

Sorcinelli, M. D. *Evaluation of Teaching Handbook.* Bloomington: Dean of Faculties Office, University of Indiana, 1986.

Tuckman, H. P. "The Academic Reward Structure in American Higher Education." In D. R. Lewis and W. E. Becker, Jr. (eds.), *Academic Rewards in Higher Education.* Cambridge, Mass.: Ballinger, 1979.

Watkins, B. T. "Colleges Urged to Avow That Teaching Is Central to Their Mission and to Take Steps to Upgrade It." *Chronicle of Higher Education,* Apr. 26, 1989, p. A13.

Wilson, R. C. *The Personal Teaching-Improvement Guides Program—A User's Manual.* Berkeley: Office of Research on Teaching Improvement and Evaluation, University of California, 1987.

CHAPTER 2

Organizational Impacts on Faculty Morale and Motivation to Teach

R. Eugene Rice
Ann E. Austin

In 1986 the American Association for Higher Education honored faculty members who "make a difference" in colleges and universities across the country. The distinctive characteristic shared by these exemplary teachers was their deep commitment to teaching and respect for the power of learning. Motivation was not an issue; these instructors were energized by their work. Educational contexts that would demoralize others became challenges for these individuals; problems were reframed as opportunities. Academic careers attract self-motivated people with a strong need for autonomy. Many of the best teachers are driven by their own curiosity and an insatiable love for learning. Yet even these individuals require an organizational environment that affirms the dignity of their work, rewards teaching, and sustains morale over time.

Our recent research on the academic workplace and efforts to evaluate programs aimed at strengthening teaching have reinforced our conviction that institutional conditions make a difference—that the organizational environment shapes faculty attitudes, perceptions, and performance. There will always be a few dedicated, heroic teachers who are so thoroughly committed to their work that even the most adverse conditions challenge them. But for most, the intrinsic characteristics of faculty work—as attractive as they are—are not enough; the intellectual challenge of teaching, the opportunity to help shape a new generation, the rewarding interactions with students do not suffice. Although important—essential, in fact—these benefits are not enough to sustain morale and keep the majority of faculty fully engaged with the process of teaching over the long term.

The general occupational climate that has so dispirited the American professoriate over the past decade and a half is on the verge of change. The 1989 Carnegie survey of 5,500 faculty indicates that faculty are gaining an increasingly positive perception of their work (Carnegie Foundation, 1989). When asked if this is a good time for a young person to begin an academic career in the United States, two-thirds of these teachers agreed. Asked the same question five years ago in the 1984 survey, only half of the faculty shared this point of view (Carnegie Foundation, 1984). In the 1989 study, 80 percent of faculty said they would become college teachers if they had it to do over again, whereas only a small number (17 percent) wished they had chosen another profession. Almost half the faculty surveyed agreed that their institution was a "very good place" to work. This represents an 8 percent improvement in the response to the same question five years earlier. Morale within the academic profession is generally on the upswing. There is considerable disparity, however, from sector to sector and institution to institution.

In this chapter, we will focus on the institutional conditions that sustain morale and motivate faculty to take teaching seriously. We want to build on our specific research projects and involvement in the evaluation of teaching-related programs in colleges and universities across the country. The first study on which we want to draw is of small liberal arts colleges. Here we were able to identify several factors that characterize colleges with high faculty morale. We will look again at these characteristics to see how they contribute to the concern for teaching. The second study we consider is an evaluation of the Lilly Endowment Program aimed at supporting teaching among junior faculty in research universities.

Our first study of exemplary liberal arts colleges allows us to examine institutional factors supporting faculty morale and teaching in colleges where teaching is the primary commitment. The second project deals with institutional settings in which teaching is not a high priority and junior faculty are systematically encouraged to attend to their research, not to their teaching.

The Liberal Arts College: Morale and Motivation

The Council of Independent Colleges (CIC) initiated a major study of the workplace in liberal arts colleges (Rice and Austin, 1988) because it was believed that morale among faculty had declined most in such colleges. The retrenchment in higher education had promised to have its most debilitating impact on the private liberal arts colleges, which heavily depended on rapidly rising tuitions. The liberal arts disciplines had also suffered decline in enrollments and prestige as students turned to career-oriented programs. Surely, faculty morale and satisfaction would be at its lowest in that particular section of higher education.

To the surprise of many, CIC's national survey of over 4,000 faculty in 140 colleges revealed that faculty morale in private, liberal arts colleges had *not* deteriorated as dramatically as expected. A number of the institutions surveyed had, in fact, remarkably high morale. In an effort to identify organizational factors contributing to good morale among faculty, we selected ten of the colleges with high scores on satisfaction and morale scales for a series of in-depth case studies. These ten included Eastern Mennonite College (Virginia), College of Notre Dame (California), Gordon College (Massachusetts), Greenville College (Illinois), Lenoir-Rhyne College (North Carolina), Nebraska Wesleyan University, Saint Scholastica College (Minnesota), Simpson College (California), Smith

College (Massachusetts), and William Jewell College (Missouri). We looked at the key organizational characteristics described in the following subsections not only for how they enhance faculty morale but also for how they motivate faculty to take teaching seriously.

Distinctive Organizational Culture. The leaders of liberal arts colleges have long been aware of the power and significance of the organizational culture of an institution. In fact, most liberal arts colleges were founded for the purpose of perpetuating a distinctive culture. Regrettably, this emphasis on the special mission of the institution has, in recent years, given way in many colleges to pragmatic concerns about basic survival and the demands of the marketplace. This is not true, however, of the above-mentioned ten colleges with high faculty morale.

The single most important hallmark of these colleges with high faculty morale is that each has a clearly articulated mission and assiduously cultivates a distinctive, coherent culture. These colleges say what they do, in very clear terms, and then they do what they say.

This cultural coherence permeates the institution. For instance, the site visitors involved in our study arrived at Gordon College very late at night and requested help from the campus security guard in finding their rooms. While escorting the visitors to their rooms, the security guard talked incessantly about the college, telling one story after another. The next day the survey team met with the chair of the board of trustees, who also told stories about the college. Most striking was that the stories of both the guard and the chair were the same. Whether talking with faculty, students, board members, or staff, the stories—the college lore—were found to be similar. In this college and others selected for study, organizational culture runs deep.

At the heart of the culture of these institutions is a firm, unswerving commitment to teaching—these are unabashedly "teaching institutions." The development of the "whole student" becomes a pivot point around which everything else revolves. For faculty, this cultural priority makes the role of teacher and the relationship to students of primary importance. Whereas faculty in other institutions struggle with the competing demands of multiple roles and ambiguous standards of evaluation, particularly surrounding the relationship between research and teaching, the faculty of these colleges know that their vocation is teaching and that this role is central to the institution. Disciplinary research, community service, and governance activities are valued but are valued in relation to this primary organizational agenda.

All but one of the ten colleges in our study are religious in character, having their culture firmly rooted in theological soil. A strong sense of history shapes their present and informs their planning for the future. Of the total 140 colleges in the CIC survey, a number have distinctive organizational cultures but high morale among faculty is lacking. What makes the ten colleges we studied stand out from the others is that their particularity—their distinctive values and commitments—is combined with openness and a genuine respect for difference. Cultural particularity can undermine faculty morale if it erodes academic freedom and discourages the critical thinking required for the intellectual and ethical development of students. Cultural distinctiveness is not enough; it is the delicate balance between particularity and openness that makes these colleges special. Faculty commitment to the college and to teaching is enhanced by an intellectual climate that values a sense of community as well as critical thought.

One of the most serious challenges for administrators in colleges of this sort is to maintain both the distinctive culture of the community and the critical thought required for the intellectual growth of students and faculty. Focusing primarily on community can lead to a stultifying parochialism and faculty stagnation. However, cultivating only the critical side—stressing pluralism and openness—can result in a kind of empty relativism in which faculty and students "talk past" one another and seldom engage intellectually or personally.

Our study of small, liberal arts colleges suggests that faculty morale and student learning are enhanced by the

creative tension between distinctive community culture and
critical thought. When the commitments underlying the community culture are openly debated in an intellectually rigor-
ous way, these concepts can be seen in context and thus
imbued with new meaning. In such a setting, teaching and
learning become especially enticing endeavors.

Distinctive organizational cultures need not be explicitly
religious. Eastern Mennonite, Nebraska Wesleyan, Saint Scholastica, and William Jewell have ties to religious communities
that are clear, direct, and thoughtfully nurtured. However, the
particularity of Smith College is based on providing a distinguished education for highly motivated, intellectually oriented
women at a time when many other women's colleges have
become coeducational. Smith's resolute focus on the education
of women is balanced by a strong emphasis on diversity and
respect for dissent. Community and critical thought coexist in
a creative tension that provides an educational environment
that is challenging to both faculty and students.

Organizational culture cannot be invented de novo nor
imposed ex cathedra. The power of organizational culture,
however, can be rejuvenated and reinforced through events
and structures that are heavily laden with the symbolic—the
stories told, the people honored, the ceremonies and rituals,
the personnel policies, and even the architecture.

The significance of faculty in the life of the institution
can be underscored in a variety of ways. The importance of
teaching can be highlighted through different forms of recognition. The schools with high faculty morale place priority
on honoring faculty. At several of these colleges, buildings on
campus are named after faculty members known to generations of students, whose lives exemplify core values of their
institution. This contrasts with the more common practice of
naming buildings after contributors. As a symbolic gesture,
this particular act gives dignity to the faculty role and is a
clear statement of institutional priorities.

Participatory Leadership. We assumed from the beginning of our study that effective leadership would be a key

factor separating those institutions with high faculty morale from those with low morale. After reviewing the literature on academic leadership, we were confident that a variety of leadership styles would work; what is important is managerial effectiveness. We assumed that some deans and presidents would be participatory in their approach and that others would be more hierarchical, depending on their abilities to be especially effective and productive.

This assumption, which we believed both reasonable and in accord with the most recent research on the subject, was not supported by the case studies. Every one of the ten colleges with high morale had leaders who were aggressively participatory. Not only were the leaders participatory in their leadership style, but the organizational structures also required active involvement of faculty in making important institutional decisions. Also of interest was that when the forty colleges in the CIC study that were in the upper range of faculty morale were compared with the forty colleges having the lowest morale, the higher-morale schools were more likely to encourage risk taking, to welcome new ideas, and were more apt to involve faculty in decision making across the board.

Our case studies reveal what on the surface appears to be a contradiction. The colleges with high morale have both strong leadership and an organizational structure that minimizes hierarchical distinctions. The visiting teams found ample evidence of creative and forceful leadership. At the same time, most of these colleges have intentionally structured a relatively flat hierarchy.

Greenville College, for instance, states explicitly in its faculty handbook that "the distinction between instruction and administration is meant to be only that of function and suggests no hierarchy of value related to the respective duties of each group." At Eastern Mennonite, this orientation is embedded in the school's Anabaptist history of brotherhood, service, and humility, which are institutionalized in a college in which leadership is widely shared and decision making is largely consensual.

In these institutions, power is not viewed as a zero-sum game. It is understood, to use the words of Kanter (1983), that "power begets power." Presidents and deans share authority and in so doing empower others and enhance the effectiveness of their organizations as a whole. The respect for faculty, and the sense of trust permeating these institutions, is fostered by the sharing of important information. Detailed data and the complexities of institutional decisions are communicated in open forums.

Because they take an active role in shaping their institutions, faculty in these ten colleges have an unusually strong identification with their schools. This identification is enhanced by minimizing professional competition and emphasizing collaboration. Our survey data show that the high-morale colleges are perceived by faculty to be much more collaborative than individualistic. During the site visits, those conducting the case studies noted the ease with which faculty and administrators worked together.

Faculty at the high-morale schools have a strong sense of ownership, feeling that their college is theirs. This sense of participation, identification, and ownership undoubtedly contributes to the high morale of faculty. We are convinced that it also strengthens the commitment to teaching in institutions in which teaching is clearly the central mission.

George Simmel, the German social theorist, drew an important distinction between authority and domination: authority is embedded in communities of mutuality and interdependence, whereas domination is hierarchical, bureaucratic, impersonal, and alienating. Administrators in our ten exemplary colleges have authority but do not dominate in Simmel's sense. Faculty-administrative relationships are described as "trusting," "open," and "fair." In no sense do the faculty feel alienated from their institutions and its leadership.

This is in sharp contrast to the majority of the American professoriate. The last two Carnegie surveys (1984, 1989) found that fully two-thirds of the faculty respondents had a negative view of the administrators in charge of their institutions. The sense of estrangement runs high, particularly in large, comprehensive institutions that are, of necessity, more bureaucratic (because of size and complexity) and adversarial in their governance. This sense of alienation from the institution and its leadership can contaminate what teachers do in the classroom and how they relate to students.

Organizational Momentum. We were surprised to find that all ten of the colleges with high faculty morale have a strong sense of momentum—they are colleges "on the move." When asked about morale on campus, faculty would frequently refer to the sense of motion permeating their institutions. At William Jewell, for instance, the college was seen as "on the upswing"; at Lenoir-Rhyne, regular reference was made to the rise in quality and the new academic standards; at Saint Scholastica, the president was given credit for a sense of "forward motion" that had changed the climate of the institution.

Over the past decade, a great deal has been written about faculty who find themselves "stuck" in midcareer. Faculty members can be full professors at the age of forty and have no place to go, remaining stuck in the same place with the same colleagues for the remainder of their careers.

Our study of liberal arts faculty suggests that an individual's sense of career momentum can be related to institutional momentum. Faculty feel stuck in their careers when they are in institutions lacking direction or movement. Faculty can be devitalized by an academic environment that is itself uninspiring and stagnant. We are reminded of Gardner's (1964, p. 7) now-famous statement that "the only stability is stability in motion."

The sense of momentum in these colleges is often sustained by collective projects that encompass the whole campus. These projects involve the faculty from the start and are collaboratively designed. Curriculum development can draw faculty in an active way into the central mission of the institution and give them a stake in its future. William Jewell and Lenoir-Rhyne both launched programs aimed at enhancing academic excellence in their respective schools. The College of Notre Dame and Smith introduced innovative programs that drew into the college new student populations. To be successful, all of these programs required the support and commitment of faculty, introduced faculty to new opportunities for growth and change, and moved the institutions ahead through collective effort.

Faculty Development Programs. The results of our study clearly showed that faculty development programs can make a significant difference. Several of the colleges selected are noted for their contribution to faculty development. The "growth contract" program developed and refined by Gordon College is a case in point. (A growth contract is a plan written by the professor that spells out objectives for self-development. The plan contains specific goals for the year, and each goal is accompanied by intended means of assessment and the necessary budget allocations.)

The faculty development activities initiated by these colleges go beyond the standard support in the form of travel funding, small grants, and sabbaticals. The institution's backing of faculty development signals its commitment to teaching and indicates the kind of teaching expected of faculty. These institutions provide intellectually challenging opportunities for teachers to become acquainted with and discuss what is known about learning. Faculty in high-morale colleges are often well acquainted with the work of Perry (1968), Kolb (1984), Schulman (1987) and others known for their work on student learning and cognitive development. Scholarship that is a part of good teaching receives recognition and support.

A Broader View of Scholarship. A final, but pivotal, characteristic of these colleges that contributes to high faculty morale is the college's enlarged view of scholarship. The dominant view in most of higher education is that scholarship is basically research—the advancement of disciplinary knowledge that is publishable in refereed journals. The ten schools in our study, in one way or another, challenge this restricted view. Faculty are required to be scholars and are accorded the dignity and recognition that goes with the title, but scholarship itself is defined more broadly. Some faculty do cutting-edge research in their disciplines and publish as is traditionally expected; others engage in more general, interpretive kinds of scholarship; they also publish, but in more popular formats. Scholarship that enriches the local community, church, and public schools is recognized, and the application of knowledge in the local setting is honored. Most important, the scholarship required to maintain good teaching on a sustained basis is valued. Meeting with colleagues to discuss how ideas are presented in class, how the metaphors and analogies used in a particular field facilitate learning or lead to confusion, and how students from diverse backgrounds "make meaning" out of what is said and done in the classroom is encouraged and supported. This broader conception of scholarship allows faculty to build on their own scholarly strengths and be rewarded for them.

In the liberal arts colleges we studied, some faculty make contributions to their disciplines, but their disciplinary careers do not compete for time with their institutional careers—the priorities are clear. The same can be said for the faculty's external careers—their consulting with outside agencies. This work is valued but primarily in relation to faculty responsibility to students and the college.

The Research University: Morale and Motivation

We now consider faculty morale and motivation to teach in a radically different organizational setting—the research university. At liberal arts colleges, where teaching is central to the institutional mission, the organizational factors that support faculty morale are linked closely to incentives that motivate faculty to take teaching seriously. In contrast, at research universities, faculty morale and teaching motivation are not necessarily correlated. In fact, efforts to encourage serious attention to teaching actually may increase tensions and diminish morale.

The primary mission of research universities typically is the pursuit and production of new knowledge in the form of traditional research projects and publications. Although good teaching usually is stated as a parallel objective, explicit and implicit signals indicate the primacy of research. Tenure decisions rest heavily on faculty research productivity and usually secondarily on teaching quality. The most respected and rewarded faculty generally are star researchers and, less often, those whose major contribution is excellent teaching. Because of these factors, faculty who respond to incentives that draw their attention to teaching may feel they are sacrificing some of the time they should devote to research efforts; thus, their morale may be shaken. On the other hand, faculty development activities focused on teaching often not only help faculty with pedagogical skills but also bring them into contact with other faculty members from across the university. For many participants, these interactions mitigate the isolation often experienced by research university faculty and therefore may enhance morale. In addition, for faculty who are trying to find ways to accommodate both teaching and research, incentives supporting teaching may be morale boosters. In sum, the relationship between faculty morale and motivation to teach is complex in the research university. Nonetheless, regardless of the impact on morale, encouragement of serious attention to teaching is important for its implications for the quality of education offered.

For the past decade and a half, the Lilly Endowment has sponsored faculty development programs to assist untenured faculty in developing their teaching expertise while they simultaneously build the research agendas expected of research university faculty. Organized at more than thirty research-oriented universities, these faculty development efforts, called Teaching Fellows Programs, have been exemplary approaches for encouraging high-quality teaching in the research university context (Austin, forthcoming). Analysis of these programs and their successes, as well as of other universities' efforts to improve teaching, suggests that several organizational factors are especially important for motivating faculty at research universities toward good teaching.

Three critical factors stand out, which include several related factors. First, as in smaller colleges, teaching must be a strongly valued institutional commitment. Second, institutional leaders must articulate the importance of high-quality teaching and take the lead in initiating institutional plans to provide incentives to motivate faculty to value teaching. Third, universities that wish to motivate faculty to take teaching seriously benefit from creating communities of faculty who share a commitment to teaching.

Strong Institutional Commitment to Teaching. A university that wants its faculty to be motivated to teach well must hold as central to the institution's mission the commitment to high-quality teaching. Faculty in research universities acutely feel strong pressure to produce research, as such widely read reports as those of Bowen and Schuster (1986) and the Carnegie Foundation attest (Boyer, 1987). General discussion of the importance of good teaching is not sufficient to counterbalance the graduate school socialization process, the usual institutional reward structures, and the prevalent university rhetoric and publicity that make clear the importance of research activity. In universities in which efforts to motivate faculty to take teaching seriously succeed, thoughtful and consistent attention is directed to symbolic reminders of the importance of teaching, to the formal and informal rewards that confirm faculty work, and to the ways in which faculty are assisted in accommodating and integrating their teaching and research activities.

Universities in which good teaching is truly an organizational commitment find ways to bring teaching issues into prominent view. The annual spring banquet at the University of Massachusetts at Amherst, called the Celebration of Teaching, is a highly successful event in the institution's Lilly Teaching Fellows Program. The featured speakers are the current seven or eight junior faculty member fellows, and they share with enthusiasm some of the discoveries from their year-long series of seminars and projects. The banquet's guest list is diverse, including state-level and institutional administrators, department chairs, faculty, and students, which reflects a shared commitment to teaching that cuts across the institution. The University of Georgia, another recipient of a Lilly Endowment grant to establish a Teaching Fellows Program, holds an annual day-long teaching conference involving a nationally known speaker and invited faculty and department chairs from across the university. Both of these programs symbolically honor teaching and emphasize the importance of discourse on teaching issues. In addition to their symbolic import, these events bring together people who share a commitment to teaching and provide a forum for sharing and debate.

A university can demonstrate its commitment to teaching in other ways as well. The publicity that surrounds teaching awards and programs on teaching conveys the degree to which this institutional mission is valued. Thorough and frequent campuswide coverage can be provided about teaching issues and programs, and faculty who receive teaching awards can be highlighted prominently in university publications. Institutional commitment to teaching also is expressed through the financial allocations made to teaching-related activities. When a university allocates resources to such support services as a teaching center, instructional design consultants, faculty development programs focused on teaching, faculty travel to teaching-related conferences, and speakers and seminars on teaching, the message is that teaching is high on the list of institutional priorities, and there is thus a strong incentive for faculty to commit themselves to teaching.

If teaching is a primary institutional goal, it should be reflected in the ways in which faculty are evaluated and rewarded. Formal and informal rewards for good teaching serve as strong incentives. Conversely, if an institution's professed interest in teaching is not consistently expressed through the evaluation and reward systems, faculty may conclude that their time should be directed toward other aspects of their work. Tenure, promotion, and salary decisions are the most obvious and formal rewards that universities offer faculty. When tenure and promotion reviews, as well as salary adjustments, include serious and thoughtful evaluation of the quality of teaching and significant weighting of the results of this evaluation along with consideration of research contributions, faculty receive a strong incentive to improve their teaching.

In addition to formal rewards, universities can show interest in teaching and offer incentives to faculty through more informal means. For example, awards for high-quality teaching—bestowed with the same respect and honor attending research awards—can serve as incentives. In some cases, however, such awards can be disincentives if, for example, the award is viewed as a dubious distinction that suggests teaching expertise has substituted for research productivity. If recipients are later denied tenure or promotion, this disincentive is reinforced. When such awards are first offered, careful selection of recipients respected for both their research and teaching contributions may counteract this danger.

Deans and department chairs should not overlook the importance of expressing appreciation and recognition when they see faculty making an extra effort or being particularly successful in teaching. Interviews conducted as part of the evaluation of the Lilly Teaching Fellows Program with faculty at such institutions as the University of Illinois, Miami University of Ohio, and the State University of New York-Buffalo clearly indicate that faculty are supported in their teaching efforts when they receive informal encouragement and positive recognition from their department chairs and deans. This kind of incentive is informal, cost free, and requires little time, yet is effective.

Universities that want to encourage excellent teaching find ways to assist faculty in integrating their teaching and research. If a university chooses to embrace excellence in both teaching and research, and if it expects each faculty member to demonstrate strength in both areas, support for faculty endeavors in teaching should not undermine research efforts, and vice versa. As part of such faculty development efforts as the Lilly Teaching Fellows Program, faculty sometimes write and publish about their teaching projects; in such cases the study of teaching leads to both classroom improvement and traditional publication. Department chairs can assist faculty by establishing teaching schedules that provide the uninterrupted blocks of time needed both for good teaching preparation and research productivity. These approaches address the reality of the research university in which teaching incentives cannot succeed if they deter a faculty member's research activity.

Supportive Institutional Leaders. Closely linked to strong institutional commitment to teaching is the role institutional leaders play in articulating and supporting this mission. Presidents, provosts, and deans can set the tone for an institutional commitment to teaching by frequently discussing the importance of teaching and by recognizing and honoring examples of teaching excellence. However, upper-level support for teaching must go beyond rhetoric to action. Examples of such action are evident at some of the universities where Lilly Teaching Fellows Programs have been most successful. Some senior administrators make special efforts to discuss teaching issues at high-level meetings and to express publicly their pleasure in and support of the Teaching Fellows Program. Some take the time to attend retreats and seminars on teaching and to meet with faculty to explore concerns about teaching. For example, Associate Provost Norman Aitken at the University of Massachusetts–Amherst personally directed that institution's Teaching Fellows Program for its first three years, fitting into his schedule regular seminar meetings, retreats, and dinners with fellows. His dedicated involvement in the program's formative years was a critical factor in fostering widespread knowledge of and respect for the program and in ensuring its continuation, supported by the university budget, after the initial grant was concluded.

Because department chairs interact regularly with their faculty colleagues and usually have some impact on faculty assignments as well as on tenure, promotion, and salary decisions, they can play an important role in providing incentive plans for good teaching. Department chairs can convey to faculty members information about how teaching efforts are valued, how time is most profitably allocated, and on what basis rewards are determined. Department chairs, usually responsible for determining teaching schedules, can organize schedules so that faculty can address both teaching and research responsibilities. Those serving as chairs can have an especially strong impact on untenured faculty, who often look for spoken and unspoken guidance about whether programs to enhance teaching are worth devoting some of their already overcommitted hours to. Without the support of department chairs, many incentives to encourage good teaching may be fruitless.

Teaching Communities and Networks. When universities encourage interactions among faculty and administrators who are committed to teaching, they provide incentives for good teaching. Through such interactions, faculty can develop communities and networks within which they affirm each other in the role of teacher and provide an example to others. Once such a group exists, deans can appoint individuals from the group to serve on institutional committees addressing teaching issues. The teaching network thus becomes the nucleus of an advocacy group for teaching.

Faculty development programs that bring a group of professors together on a regular basis to address teaching issues are a very effective way to develop a cadre of teaching-oriented faculty. The Lilly Teaching Fellows Program typically involves a group of six to eight untenured faculty who individually work on course design or other teaching-related projects and collectively meet regularly, in afternoon or evening meetings or in weekend retreats, to discuss selected teaching issues. Some programs, such as those at Miami University and at the University of Georgia, include senior faculty who serve as mentors to their junior colleagues. Others, such as the long-standing University of Rhode Island program, include both senior and junior faculty in each year's selected group. In addition to the Lilly model, other structured programs also include faculty groups that meet regularly for lunch to discuss teaching issues and seminar groups that address specified topics over the course of a term. Retreats and meetings scheduled around dinner or lunch foster a sense of community among regular attendees. Over time, relationships deepen in ways that invite more open sharing of concerns and ideas about teaching and that support faculty eager to take risks and explore new approaches.

Although less regular activities involving different faculty members at each gathering are not as effective in building a sense of shared commitment, such events as occasional seminars or presentations by respected speakers to which all university faculty are invited still create informal networks. Professors interacting at such events find others who have similar concerns.

Involving faculty leaders known for their good teaching sends the message that teaching programs and seminars are not designed to be remedial for faculty having problems in the classroom. Most universities in which the Lilly Teaching Fellows Program has been established have made participation as a fellow an honor; selection and involvement in the program bring recognition and prestige.

Organizational Leadership, Morale, and Motivation

Fifteen years ago, when faculty development was emerging as a primary concern, efforts to strengthen faculty morale and to improve the quality of teaching were intentionally placed on the periphery of institutional agendas. The focus was primarily on teaching improvement strategies and personal consultations; priority was given to confidentiality and work with individuals. The faculty development office was usually located in an obscure part of the campus, where faculty could go unobtrusively to find personal assistance, and was far removed from centers of decision making and institutional power.

More recently, faculty development has become a more focal concern, and the emphasis is less on the individual than on the organization. No longer is the concern for morale and teaching improvement an entity relegated to the edge of campus; instead, it is a driving force in efforts to maintain institutional vitality.

Deans and department chairs are now considered to play a major role in maintaining faculty morale and the quality of teaching; both concerns are organizational issues. For both small liberal arts colleges and large research universities much depends on the congruence between institutional mission and what individual faculty are, in fact, rewarded for doing. Faculty will respond to institutionalized incentives. The question is "What is rewarded?" Faculty in our liberal arts colleges with high morale are strongly committed to teaching because that commitment is continually reinforced. Morale is high because there is congruence between institutional mission, rewards, and individual priorities.

The dominant incentives at the research university pull in another direction—toward research. Strong leadership firmly in support of the teaching mission of the institution is necessary as a countervailing force. A prestigious program like the Lilly Teaching Fellows Program can make a difference. This kind of extraordinary intervention is required, in fact, if quality teaching is to be more the rule than the exception.

In the research university, as well as the liberal arts college, there needs to be clarity about the teaching mission of the institution. Research universities have insisted, over the years, on maintaining large undergraduate enrollments. If teaching is not taken seriously, the "piggy-backing" of faculty research and graduate education on college enrollments becomes morally indefensible. The teaching mission needs to be affirmed by influential administrators. Organizational policies—particularly as regards reward systems—must provide clear, consistent, and real (not merely rhetorical) support for the institution's commitment to excellence in teaching. Imaginative administrative leadership and appropriate institutional incentives can make an enormous difference in improving the quality of teaching.

References

Austin, A. E. *Report* on the Lilly Teaching Fellows Program, sponsored by the Lilly Endowment, forthcoming.

Bowen, H. R., and Schuster, J. H. *American Professors: A National Resource Imperiled.* New York: Oxford University Press, 1986.

Boyer, E. L. *College: The Undergraduate Experience in America.* New York: Harper & Row, 1987.

Carnegie Foundation for the Advancement of Teaching. "National Survey of Faculty." Technical report. Washington, D.C.: Carnegie Foundation for the Advancement of Teaching, 1984.

Carnegie Foundation for the Advancement of Teaching. "Condition of the Professoriate." Technical report. Washington, D.C.: Carnegie Foundation for the Advancement of Teaching, 1989.

Gardner, J. *Self-Renewal.* New York: Harper & Row, 1964.

Kanter, R. M. *Change Masters.* New York: Simon & Schuster, 1983.

Kolb, D. A. *Experiential Learning: Experience as the Source of Learning and Development.* Englewood Cliffs, N.J.: Prentice-Hall, 1984.

Perry, W. G., Jr. *Forms of Intellectual and Ethical Development in the College Years: A Scheme.* New York: Holt, Rinehart & Winston, 1968.

Rice, R. E., and Austin, A. E. "High Faculty Morale: What Exemplary Colleges Do Right." *Change,* 1988, *20* (2), 50–58.

Schulman, L. "Knowledge and Teaching: Foundation of the New Reform." *Harvard Educational Review,* 1987, *57* (1), 1–22.

PART TWO

The Administrator's Role in Strengthening Instructional Quality

CHAPTER 3

Why Good Teaching
Needs Active Leadership
Madeleine F. Green

It is rare that administrators simply *make* something happen, especially if that something affects the faculty. Some administrators believe that they have a very limited role to play in improving teaching. As one administrator put it, "There is relatively little an administrator can do. . . . The faculty member simply has to be motivated." Although some are more sanguine about the potential for administrative leadership, this assertion rings true. It is an unqualified description of the limitations of administrative power. Who could imagine a faculty happily accepting a pronouncement from the dean or president about the core curriculum or about requirements for the major? That is not how we do business in academia.

Indeed, the current climate in higher education works against heroic leadership. Vocal and multiple constituencies, increased intervention by state boards, system offices, and accrediting bodies, unionization, and a litigious climate have decreased leaders' latitude in decision making. Some claim that today's leaders have been reduced to mere managers and consensus builders (Fisher, 1984; Commission on Strengthening Presidential Leadership, 1984).

However, if there really were no possibility of accomplishing anything, surely there would be far fewer applicants for administrative positions. For the best administrators, the hope of making a difference, leaving "one's thumbprint" lures them to the job (Gardner, 1987, p. 16). Deans and academic vice-presidents can cause things to happen—planting ideas, nurturing them, soliciting support from faculty leaders, and pushing ideas through an often tortuous route of dialogue and revision until these ideas are ultimately owned by the affected groups. In other words, in academia, leaders (faculty or administrators) can influence the organizational culture to produce change. One president articulated this notion as follows: "I don't accept the notion that presidents can't influence teaching. They can create a climate where certain things are apt to happen. . . . Presidents have a great deal of power in choosing the direction of a university, in creating a climate. Faculty will respond."

The Context of Change

Change occurs in the context of an institution's values, norms, traditions, and history—its culture. Leadership, then, involves not simply having ideas and implementing them "but also interpreting and communicating institutional values and understanding organizational processes" (Chaffee and Tierney, 1988, p. 3). As most successful leaders realize, perhaps intuitively, there must be a match between the leader's vision and the environment. If there is a mismatch or if leaders violate the institution's cultural norms, conflict generally ensues. The leader is forcibly reminded that he or she has transgressed the bounds of the institution's norms.

An institution's culture is shaped by many factors, some of them external. National demographics, the political climate, and the economic picture will be important factors in defining an institution's current situation. As we look at these factors, several are especially relevant to the issue of teaching.

The Aging Work Force. The aging of faculty, administrators, and staff brings into sharp relief issues of professional vitality and motivation. More people will be at their jobs longer, and the challenge for faculty will be to stay interested, up to date, and lively in their professions. We will need new definitions of academic careers. A career in academe need not be a lifetime commitment. It is already the case that in some fields, faculty spend periods of time in corporations, in laboratories, and as consultants. The beneficial effects of changing environments, breaking from the routine of teaching and university life, are abundant. Academic administrators will need to think differently about the academic profession, including who teaches, for how long, and in what way.

The Plateauing Phenomenon. Bardwick (1986) describes the phenomenon of reaching a plateau in one's work life as largely a function of structure; that is, plateauing occurs when employees cannot move upward in the organization. The combination of steady state or decline and an aging work force makes this a relatively new phenomenon in corporations. In academe, the plateaued professor is not new; forty-year teaching careers are not unusual. Today, however, faculty have fewer alternatives within the academy. It is difficult to move to another institution unless one is a "superstar" or in a high-demand field; moving into the administrative ranks may be unlikely owing to congestion in that area. Moving out of academe is not easily done or encouraged in some fields. Thus, finding meaning and challenge in a stable teaching career, creating a "feeling of movement," is not easy (Bardwick, 1986, p. 15).

Changing Work Values. Faculty have always laid a strong claim to participation in decision making on campus. These claims have been intensified by changes in social character that have affected American society since the 1960s (Maccoby, 1988). Increased emphasis on leisure time, self-fulfillment, and increased affluence have raised expectations of job satisfaction. Bureaucracy bashing from the left and the right has decreased everyone's tolerance of traditional bureaucratic decision making. Questioning of authority and the assertion of individual rights are an integral part of our current value system. These changing work values are important determinants of institutional culture.

New Students. Increased numbers of minority, older, part-time, and underprepared students are changing the face of higher education. A changed student population calls for a basic redefinition of academic programs, administrative structures, and, in some cases, institutional philosophy. If higher education is to serve these students, we will need to enhance our understanding of pedagogy, encourage flexible teaching styles, and value and reward good teaching. It is not enough to open the doors; we know now that it is not possible to make all students fit the mold of a traditional university. Now is the time for institutions to change. A significant share of the burden of change will fall on faculty; the teaching-and-learning processes are the core of student success. Administrators will also play an important role in shaping the institutional structures and policies that define the environment for students and faculty.

Accountability. The ongoing debate on quality and assessment is likely to be prominent for the foreseeable future. Increased pressures from students as consumers, from state legislators, and from parents paying ever increasing tuition will intensify the need for faculty to take an active role in controlling the quality of the classroom experience. For administrators, the challenge will be to provide leadership in this traditional bastion of faculty hegemony. Accountability can easily turn into an adversarial proposition. Unless faculty share the idea that assessment and accountability are potentially positive educational forces rather than administrative nuisances or merely political ploys, real accountability will not happen. Instead, the definition of quality will be peripheral, failing to get at the heart of the matter.

Leadership Tasks

The relationship between institutional leaders and culture is reciprocal: leaders are not simply constrained by institutional values and norms; they are in a position to shape them through words and deeds. Since administrators cannot simply legislate good teaching, what can they do to support, celebrate, and reward it? What are the tasks of leaders that are especially important to accomplishing these goals?

Symbolic Leadership. Symbolism is a vital aspect of leadership, whether the leader is a community activist, political figure, or college administrator. Academic leaders embody the values and aspirations of the college and its constituents, who in turn project their hopes and goals on to leaders. The symbolic dimension of leadership has always been important, but it is even more so now, given the fragmentation that characterizes many of our institutions today. On some campuses, where the sense of community and unity is strong (such as church-related or historically black institutions), the leader is often invested with the shared energy and collective goals of the group. To the extent that the communal agenda holds together, the leader retains the symbolic power vested in him or her by the campus community. However, when consensus is minimal, the leader's mandate is less clear. He or she will symbolize different things to different people. Finding opportunities to strengthen the collective vision and to articulate shared goals is clearly a challenge for leaders today.

How does symbolic leadership become operational? A leader's actions and words have symbolic as well as overt meaning. Deans who teach, presidents who walk around campus and meet faculty in their offices, department chairs who involve the senior faculty in teaching lower-level courses all make statements that go beyond the actual deeds. Symbolic leadership from the top is especially important in effecting change. Presidents who are committed to a pluralistic campus send powerful messages when their own staff and senior officers reflect the diversity they would have the rest of the campus embody. Similarly, good teaching will not become a high priority unless academic leaders articulate and consistently reinforce it.

Symbolic gestures, complemented by concrete actions,

are important means of changing an institutional culture. A number of symbolic acts can convey that teaching is highly valued. Establishing a tradition of awarding the title of "professor of the year" is one such example. This award can be a meaningful ritual, or it can be a perfunctory exercise. Do the deans and the president take an active role in publicizing the award? Does the ritual surrounding its conferral serve to rally the academic community? Are the rewards meaningful? Does the institution make an effort to capitalize on the skills of that excellent teacher?

The University of Colorado recently created a Presidential Teaching Scholars Program designed to identify and recognize excellent teachers, to improve the instructional skills of the faculty, and to develop the group of recognized teachers into "a sustaining cadre who will serve as advocates and consultants for teaching excellence in University programs" (University of Colorado, public announcement, April 1989). The teaching scholars will receive a $4,000 stipend of unrestricted compensation and $2,000 for a development account. They will "be used by the president for advice, consultation, and advocacy of continuing efforts to recognize, reward, and promote the teaching mission of the university. They will serve as a mentor to a junior faculty member and, in conjunction with the director of the Teaching Excellence Program at the Boulder campus, will develop activities including a retreat, videotaping of classes, and consultation." The active presidential interest apparent in this program suggests that its effect can be as symbolic as it is real. The nomination and selection process, involving multiple campus groups, also has the potential of capturing the interest and enthusiasm of faculty and students.

Many institutions have teaching awards. Professor-of-the-year awards are one illustrative example of a new effort to put teaching higher up on the institution's symbolic agenda. However, there are dangers to such programs. For example, an annual award in a small college with little faculty turnover will soon lose its impact. One administrator described some faculty members as campaigning for the award. Also, symbolic gestures must have real meaning. Monetary rewards, widespread recognition, and opportunities to capitalize on recognized teaching talents are important methods of making symbolic gestures real. And, certainly, considering teaching to be a meaningful criterion for promotion and tenure is vital in reinforcing the symbolic recognition of good teaching. A high profile and sustained support from leaders are important ingredients for the success of such ventures.

Symbols become real when an institution is willing to spend money for them. George Mason University has fourteen endowed Robinson Professorships. These star professors are teacher/scholars who are doing broadly integrative work that does not fit neatly into one discipline. Rather, their *raison* is to teach interdisciplinary courses to undergraduates and to improve undergraduate teaching.

The behaviors of individual administrators have a symbolic function as well. In many institutions, it is a real struggle for administrators to continue teaching or writing; the demands of their positions are simply too great. Yet most deans and chief academic officers say that it is a good idea to try to keep their hand in one or both areas—through team teaching, taking responsibility for a portion of a course, or taking time in their schedule to read and write.

Certainly, any administrative initiative or statement can have a symbolic value. What is important for change is the leader's ability to understand and interpret the institutional culture and through the deliberate use of symbols—language, mottos, traditions, rituals, and new initiatives, to name a few— to create a climate that can internalize and accept change.

Coalition Building. Campuses are fragmented in a number of ways. Faculty, students, parents, legislators, trustees, alumni, and the community are stakeholders with different perspectives and values. There is also competition within the campus community to gain importance on the institution's agenda (Green, 1988). Symbolic leadership is one way to create a community from disparate groups and interests; building coalitions and consensus is another.

Creating support for good teaching requires mobilization of students, faculty, department chairs, and administrators. Students may be more interested in getting by or getting good grades; faculty might prefer to concentrate on research or service. The notion that teaching is a private matter between teachers and their students has many adherents in the professoriate, and the assertion that this transaction should be subject to scrutiny by colleagues and chairs is not universally welcome. In short, making teaching a shared priority requires articulating the vision, getting others to accept it, and then working together to make it happen.

It is worth reminding ourselves that good teaching is a motherhood-and-apple-pie issue—no one is against it. The problem lies with overcoming fear of change, inertia, and the fact that faculty priorities may be elsewhere. Building coalitions entails creating a momentum for change. It is easy to pay lip service to the importance of teaching but a considerable effort to mobilize people is required to make this a priority.

The task of coalition building is often unobtrusive, requiring that administrators move quietly behind the scenes to resolve conflicts and overcome inertia. This is a nonheroic role (Green, 1988); the administrator must convince, cajole, reward, and promote cooperation. Coalition and consensus building is one of the most important tasks of academic administrators. Leaders with high ego needs or an inability to listen to competing views will have difficulty fulfilling this task. Heroic leadership does not necessarily mobilize faculty. Charismatic leadership may galvanize them, but if the leader's message falls on deaf ears, the result may be resistance (passive or active) rather than enthusiasm. It is one thing to have vision or, in less grandiose terms, a sense of where an institution ought to be heading. It is quite another to enlist those who must believe in the vision and "own" it in order to implement it.

Change at the grass-roots level is essential. Lindquist (1980) suggests the creation of networks of people on campus who are linked to each other and to resources outside the institution that can help them improve teaching and learning. These networks link professors with each other through the development of teams and provide the information needed to address these issues. The resources include information on teaching and learning available through publications, visits to other campuses, and attendance at conferences and workshops. An example of such a network is the University of Wisconsin's Faculty College, a four-day workshop that provides an opportunity for faculty members from each of the fifteen member institutions to join together for intensive study and discussion in an attempt to improve undergraduate education. Sponsored by the university's Undergraduate Teaching Improvement Council, this workshop is offered once a year.

Another such network is the Washington Center for Improving the Quality in Undergraduate Education. Based at Evergreen State College in Olympia, Washington, this clearinghouse has "coordinated the development of course designs used by thirty-seven public and private colleges and universities, including twenty-two of the state's twenty-six community colleges" (Monaghan, 1989, p. 11). The clearinghouse helps faculty from these different institutions collaborate on innovative curricula and course designs, stresses collaborative teaching, and facilitates faculty exchanges.

Faculty Leadership. Change can be initiated by top leadership, but to endure, change requires leadership from the ranks. Responsibility for academic leadership does not rest with deans and vice-presidents alone. Well-respected senior faculty are generally powerful figures and can choose to champion or derail initiatives for change. Similarly, an enthusiastic and committed associate dean who follows through on faculty suggestions or a director of faculty development who is held in high esteem by peers is also critical to a successful effort to improve teaching.

Many programs to support the improvement of teaching rely heavily on senior faculty. A program at the California State University–Long Beach, funded by the Fund for the

Improvement of Postsecondary Education, matched senior faculty with new faculty in a mentoring program. The pairs meet regularly to discuss issues related to teaching, publications, and the promotion and tenure process. They also meet monthly as a group, having varying agendas, or "miniworkshops," on relevant topics. Now in its second year, the project has received very positive reviews from the participants. Benefits accrue to both new faculty and the mentors. In their evaluation study of the project, Boice and Turner (1989, p. 14) cite several benefits to the participants who "consistently reported delight in rediscovering that mentoring is much more than just altruism. They felt that they benefited at least as much on finding new friendship and in formulating new plans to revitalize their own teaching and scholarship."

The University of Georgia is launching a Senior Fellows Teaching Program, the goal of which is "to increase the prestige of undergraduate instruction and improve the quality of instruction provided to undergraduates at UGA by increasing the involvement of experienced senior faculty" (University of Georgia, preliminary proposal, n.d.). These faculty will serve as mentors to junior faculty in their departments and participate in the training of teaching assistants. The eight fellows selected each year will receive "release time, financial resources, and training necessary to plan and implement substantial improvements in a significant lower-division undergraduate course or course sequence in their disciplines." William Jackson, associate director of the Office of Instructional Development, cites three factors that are important to the development of a successful program (correspondence with the author, April 26, 1989). First is the support of the highest levels of administration. The Office of Instructional Development reports directly to the vice-president for academic affairs. "Credibility with and input from the faculty" is a second factor; the Office of Instructional Development is supported by a universitywide faculty committee. Third is a broad-based institutional approach to "develop a climate that encourages and rewards effective teaching."

Sharing responsibility means sharing information and authority. Plante (cited in Green, 1988, p. 83) advises administrators to "seek their faculty's advice on all significant issues, especially those involving personnel and fiscal matters, and use their faculty's initiatives as part of the institution's strategic planning."

Shared decision making is a long-standing value in the academy. It was a value in the academic culture long before it was "discovered" by the corporate sector, which looked to Japan for its "new" models of worker involvement. Theoretical models and research have validated what academics have always known intuitively. Studies by Vroom and Jago (1988, p. 57) show that "participation tends to produce feelings of acceptance and joint ownership over the decision" and that more participation in the formulation of a decision is required if it is to be widely accepted. Participatory decision making takes longer, but the investment of time enhances the possibility of making the idea a shared goal.

Why is empowering leaders throughout the institution relevant to the goal of improving teaching? Making good teaching an institutional priority requires changing values, behaviors, and academic norms. Graduate school socializes students to the research component of the professorial job. Few graduate programs include courses about teaching in the discipline or pose questions on the nature of inquiry in the discipline. Professors do not automatically place a high priority on teaching or know how to be effective in the classroom. As teaching institutions aspire to greater national recognition and excellence, research is emphasized for promotion and tenure at the expense of teaching. Finding these incongruities and making them explicit are important steps in changing institutional culture.

Mobilizing faculty leaders to take the initiative for change may require creating new structures, programs, or task forces. Or, if ineffective structures exist, these may need to be reenergized by new leadership or new ideas. If faculty are to exert real leadership, they must have the power to get things done and the necessary resources to do so.

Recommendations for Administrators

Recommending strategies for improving some aspect of institutional performance is always risky. The preceding pages have emphasized the importance of recognizing institutional culture as a dynamic partner in leadership, each shaping the other. No two institutions are alike; therefore, no two would employ all the same strategies for change. Differences among institutions with respect to valuing and rewarding teaching are especially pronounced. Research institutions have a clear ethos of research first; many undergraduate institutions, and certainly community colleges, are committed to teaching in word and in deed. Most institutions are chronically ambivalent. The following recommendations are framed for institutions that are struggling to put teaching higher on their agendas, that acknowledge that teaching is "the business of the business" (Zemsky, 1989, p. 1) but whose practices and reward systems send a different message.

In spite of the differences among institutions, some strategies will work some of the time for some institutions. The following principles and strategies are presented in this spirit:

1. *Make good teaching a leadership priority.* Chairs, deans, and vice-presidents have multiple opportunities to articulate institutional priorities (see Rice and Austin, this volume). The process of creating a different climate requires that the new values and priorities be articulated forcefully and repeatedly. Convocations, faculty meetings, and retreats of various groups provide forums for introducing and reinforcing institutional change.

2. *Be a partner in the venture.* Make every effort to teach if you are an administrator below the presidential level. (Teaching is rarely feasible for chief executive officers.) Doing so is a symbol of your identification with the faculty and shows that you care enough to make teaching a priority. More important, it involves you as an administrator in the real world of the teaching. However, do not commit yourself to more than you can realistically do. It is worse to keep

cancelling classes or be unresponsive to students than to not teach at all.

3. *Have faculty lead the charge.* The nature of the academic enterprise is such that faculty will generally disparage or resist administrative leadership. Leadership from peers on issues that affect the daily lives of faculty is likely to be more palatable. Academic administrators who want to foster good teaching must be serious about listening to the faculty about how this can be accomplished and must be prepared to do it their way, within reason. This does not mean that administrators should abdicate their role as leaders; rather, to empower others is an act of leadership.

4. *Put your money where your rhetoric is.* Nothing produces cynicism and apathy in faculty faster than administrators who pay lip service to one thing (such as faculty participation or good teaching) but whose actions contradict their rhetoric. Innovations usually have a price tag, and it would be foolish to undertake a change in the institutional value system without investing some money and time. Release time for faculty, making information available, and enabling faculty to attend conferences and visit other campuses have attendant costs. Be prepared to support these actions, verbally and financially.

5. *Reward good teaching in ways that matter.* Here is a distressingly familiar obstacle and one that is central to the success of any attempt to improve teaching. Institutions often do not value good teaching enough to make it a serious consideration in the promotion and tenure process. A plaque for good teaching is not helpful to an individual who is denied tenure. If teaching does not really count significantly, then it is professional suicide for a junior faculty member to concentrate on doing more than being an acceptable teacher. While it is not life threatening to senior faculty, in the sense that their jobs do not depend on keeping their noses to the research grindstone, the intrinsic rewards of being good at one's craft may not be sufficient incentive for all; professors are not saints. In short, as Seldin (this volume) points out, if institutions do not seriously reward good teaching in deed

as well as in word, good teaching will not occur as often as it should.

6. *Encourage life outside the department.* External resources and stimuli are very helpful. Dialogues across the disciplines shed new perspectives on one's field. An appreciation for the total educational process helps put one's discipline and courses in perspective. Some work on pedagogy is discipline specific, but it is also helpful to know that other faculty members struggle with the same issues and have different insights based on their experiences and intellectual vistas.

7. *Encourage contacts outside the institution.* Good teaching is a growth industry in higher education. Publications, conferences, and workshops on the topic abound. Off-campus activities involving people from other institutions have multiple payoffs. First, one gains factual information on how others are doing things. Second, there is the benefit of knowing that widespread attention is being paid to the issue; it is not simply an aberrant crusade of the current administration. Third, the network of people and resources can endure long after the conference is over. The effect of all these activities can be a rekindling of a teacher's enthusiasm for an undertaking that requires sustained and fatiguing attention.

8. *Define teaching broadly.* Teaching is not limited to the classroom. Professors can teach in the community by giving talks to high schools, clubs, and civic organizations. They can teach by sharing with their colleagues. Teaching is sharing all we know with those who want to learn (P. Plante, personal communication, Apr. 24, 1989). Similarly, teaching and scholarship need not be viewed as parallel but nonintersecting activities. Boyer (1987, p. 131) notes that "scholarship is not an esoteric appendage; it is at the heart of what the profession is all about." Faculty must keep learning in order to stay vital. Scholarship is not necessarily limited to publications in refereed journals. Staying abreast of the developments in the discipline, participating in disciplinary meetings, and incorporating new knowledge into the curriculum are also forms of scholarship. If teaching is broadly defined as involv-

ing students, the public, and scholarship, professors have multiple sources from which to draw intellectual energy.

9. *Work from an understanding of adult development.* Faculty careers evolve, and junior faculty have very different needs than those of senior professors. For junior faculty, the issue may be their socialization to the norms and expectations of the institution. For older colleagues, the need may be to branch out or to serve as mentor to a junior member. Some institutions have formalized programs wherein senior faculty who are well respected for teaching serve as mentors. Also, breaking the monotony of a repetitive full-time teaching load through special assignments, release time, or administrative internships may help energize a midlife professor.

10. *Make good teaching an institutional responsibility not simply an individual one.* Traditionally, the burden of faculty and administrative development has been on the individual. As the student population becomes more diverse, with differing levels of preparation and learning styles, the teaching task becomes more complicated and the ability of the individual to deal with such complexity becomes more limited. If they are to serve new populations of students, institutions will have to pay attention to helping faculty recognize and adapt to their students' differences. These efforts serve everyone's best interests—the institution, the faculty, and the students.

11. *Make teaching ability a criterion for hiring faculty.* Most of the preceding recommendations deal with faculty already at the institution. The next twenty years will see accelerated retirements and hiring. Certainly, hiring good teachers to begin with may be the most important intervention of all, but it is difficult to assess a candidate's teaching ability. Every effort should be made by departments to judge a candidate's teaching effectiveness, and it should be a clear criterion for hiring.

Conclusion

Faculty development and the encouragement of good teaching are not new issues. They are newly important, however, because many factors have conspired in the past twenty-five years to push the issue lower down on institutions' agendas. The growing importance of research in garnering institutional support has made research a dominant element in defining excellence for many campuses. Even those campuses that recognize teaching as their central mission are tempted to use the yardstick of research productivity and external support as indices of faculty and institutional quality. As many institutions drift away from emphasizing teaching, caught up in the national competition of a single model of excellence, pressures mount to serve the needs of new populations of students and to demonstrate greater accountability to students, parents, and taxpayers concerning the quality of the education delivered. This collision of mission and expectations has engendered a heightened interest in improving teaching.

The issue may be familiar, but the context described above is a product of this particular moment in time. Thus, administrators must take a fresh look at an enduring problem. Some of the strategies to improve teaching will be familiar; others will be anchored in the circumstances that have given rise to the current preoccupation. In the current climate of fragmentation of campus interests and widening gulfs between faculty members seeking autonomy and administrators preoccupied with accountability and prudent management, administrators will need to make careful judgments about exercising leadership. The balance between articulating a new vision and leading without followers, between raising aspirations and going on a fool's errand, is not an obvious one. Administrators will need to take a careful reading of their environments to orchestrate the process of change.

References

Bardwick, J. *The Plateauing Trap.* New York: AMACOM, American Management Association, 1986.

Bennis, W., and Nanus, B. *Leaders.* New York: Harper & Row, 1985.

Boice, R., and Turner, J. L. "The Fund for the Improvement

of Postsecondary Education—California State University–Long Beach Mentoring Project for New Faculty." Long Beach: Center for Faculty Development, California State University–Long Beach, 1989.

Boyer, E. L. *College: The Undergraduate Experience in America.* New York: Harper & Row, 1987.

Chaffee, E., and Tierney, W. *Collegiate Culture and Leadership Strategies.* New York: American Council on Education/Macmillan, 1988.

Commission on Strengthening Presidential Leadership. *Presidents Make a Difference: Strengthening Leadership in Colleges and Universities.* Washington, D.C.: Association of Governing Boards of Universities and Colleges, 1984.

Fisher, J. *The Power of the Presidency.* New York: American Council on Education/Macmillan, 1984.

Gardner, J. W. *Attitudes and Context.* Leadership Papers no. 6. Washington, D.C.: Independent Sector, 1987.

Green, M. F. "Toward a New Leadership Model." In M. F. Green (ed.), *Leaders for a New Era: Strategies for Higher Education.* New York: American Council on Education/Macmillan, 1988.

Kerr, C., and Gade, M. L. *The Many Lives of Academic Presidents.* Washington, D.C.: Association of Governing Boards of Universities and Colleges, 1986.

Lindquist, J. "Improving the Teaching-Learning Environment." In P. Jedamus, M. W. Peterson, and Associates (eds.), *Improving Academic Management: A Handbook of Planning and Institutional Research.* San Francisco: Jossey-Bass, 1980.

Maccoby, M. *Why Work: Leading the New Generation.* New York: Simon & Schuster, 1988.

Monaghan, P. "Unusual Washington State Clearinghouse Develops Teaching-and-Learning Innovation for Colleges." *Chronicle of Higher Education,* June 7, 1989, pp. 11–13.

Plante, P. "In Support of Faculty Leadership." In M. F. Green (ed.), *Leaders for a New Era: Strategies for Higher Education.* New York: American Council on Education/Macmillan, 1988.

Vroom, V. H., and Jago, A. G. *The New Leadership: Managing Participation in Organizations.* Englewood Cliffs, N.J.: Prentice-Hall, 1988.

Zemsky, R. "The Business of the Business." *Policy Perspectives,* 1989, *1* (3), 1-7.

CHAPTER 4

The Department Chair as Change Agent

Ann F. Lucas

Deans and vice-presidents of academic affairs in colleges and universities all over the country are becoming increasingly concerned about the quality of teaching in their institutions. Academic chairs, who are feeling the impact of increasing accountability, share such concerns about teaching effectiveness (Lucas, 1989b). Yet many chairs feel they can do little to improve teaching. This is especially true in unionized institutions in which chairs, as faculty, are part of the bargaining unit. In such situations, chairs wonder if they have any right or power to try to change colleagues' behavior. Thus, the conflict that chairs have always felt inherent in the dual role of being both a member of the faculty and of the administration is exacerbated by the pressure they feel from deans and other academic leaders to do something to improve teaching in their departments.

On the national level, enhancing the quality of teaching has become a central issue for professional organizations of higher education. The fact that the theme of AAHE conferences for the past six years has been quality teaching reflects this interest. During this same six-year period, numerous reports and publications have been highly critical of the quality of higher education (Bennett, 1986, 1984; Boyer, 1987;

Bloom, 1987; Clark, 1987; Hirsch, 1987; Mangan, 1987; National Institute of Education, 1984; Newman, 1985). One of higher education's most severe critics, former secretary of education William Bennett (1986, p. 16), has charged that there is far too much poor teaching, not enough concern for the intellectual growth of students, and a "collective loss of nerve and faith" among faculty members and administrators of many of the nation's universities. Others agree. Frank Newman (1985, p. 23), senior author of the Carnegie Foundation's 1985 study comments with devastating candor, "College education is nowhere near as exciting or as effective as it could be. In many ways it is boring, particularly the classroom part."

Demoralized faculty members in higher education are experiencing difficulties as the rules of the only game they know rapidly change (McMillen, 1987; Seldin, 1987). While colleges and universities repeatedly intone the value of high-quality teaching, emphasis on research and publication is increasing (Seldin, 1984). It is not surprising that the 1987 Council of Independent Colleges report indicated that faculty morale seems to be highest in colleges in which (1) teaching is greatly valued, (2) a clear sense of mission exists, (3) faculty feel they have a meaningful role in governance, and (4) scholarship rather than research and publication is rewarded (Rice and Austin, 1987).

Improvement of instructional effectiveness has become the primary focus of faculty development offices. Their sophisticated, knowledgeable staffs have created a variety of programs to improve the teaching-learning process. Yet the impact of these programs on the total faculty has often not been very significant. Some faculty members, comfortable in the way they have been teaching, feel they do not have the time to examine and improve teaching when promotions and merit increases depend primarily on research and publication. Others, convinced that they are already doing a good job, see no reason to attend workshops on teaching. Cross (1977, p. 10), drawing from her self-assessment survey of college teachers, notes, "An amazing 94 percent rate themselves as above-average teachers, and 68 percent rank themselves in the top quarter in teaching performance.''

Nonetheless, instruction in American higher education needs improvement. Faculty members require support, encouragement, and sometimes an increased understanding of the teaching-learning process. Curriculum should be reshaped, and the academic environment itself requires conscious nurturing.

In this chapter, it is argued that academic chairs are the key agents for enhancing the quality of undergraduate education and that department chairs can be most effective when they are supported by academic administrators who are working toward the same goals and who agree on appropriate strategies for improving teaching. To effect educational reform, chairs must view their leadership role as different and must develop specific plans for making teaching a valued activity in the department.

Experiences of Department Chairs

In a survey administered during workshops in higher educational leadership I have conducted during the past three years, more than 1,000 department chairs were asked to indicate on a five-point scale how successful they had been in dealing with a number of faculty development problems. About three-fifths of them indicated that they were unsuccessful or very unsuccessful in at least one of the following areas: improving the overall teaching effectiveness in the department, improving the quality of performance of those who are poor teachers, motivating alienated tenured faculty, or motivating burned-out faculty members. Each of these issues is addressed in the following sections, and recommendations are made for ways to creatively adapt individual leadership styles to these situations.

One of the most difficult tasks for many chairs is that of motivating faculty. The oft-repeated cry of "How do you motivate faculty, particularly alienated, tenured faculty, when you have neither carrots nor sticks?" reflects the feeling of powerlessness more prevalent in higher education than in other organizations.

However, organizational climates that reflect such an attitude of hopelessness can be changed. And faculty, after all, are people who respond to some of the same incentives that have been found useful with individuals in other organizations. Individuals are highly motivated when they feel they are part of an important ongoing enterprise and that their participation makes a difference. Certainly, educating students can be an exciting, sometimes totally absorbing enterprise. But it can also be a tiring and, at times, frustrating experience. Teaching for its own sake is not enough of an incentive for most teachers.

Although many faculty came to higher education because they thought it was an important way in which to spend their lives, these same faculty members often feel they are not making an important difference. Many students with limited academic skills have been entering colleges in recent years. One national survey showed that the average high school student graduates with better than a B average and yet reads below the eighth-grade level (Roueche, Baker, and Roueche, 1984). Moreover, students often lack much motivation to learn the subject. Professors are fully aware that students' highest priorities do not necessarily include attending class on a regular basis or completing assigned work. Therefore, to prevent discouragement and burn-out, faculty need to function in a department that provides a supportive climate, one that encourages faculty to share recommendations for motivating students and to develop innovative strategies when the teaching situation seems desperate.

Although most faculty are experts in their disciplines, they have had no formal training in how to teach. Russell Edgerton (1988, p. B2), president of the American Association for Higher Education, underscored this problem, commenting, "Faculty members come to us strong in content and blissfully ignorant of anything having to do with theories of learning and strategies of teaching rooted in pedagogical knowledge. In their knowledge of their disciplines . . . they stand on the shoulders of giants; in their knowledge of teaching, they stand on the ground."

Thus, the department chair is in the best position to create a climate in which teaching is valued—one that makes it possible for faculty to increase their knowledge about how adults learn and what teaching strategies are effective. There is an abundance of literature on the topic of human learning and motivation and its implications for teaching. Faculty members who feel they are already knowledgeable about teaching can resist or deny this aid. This denial is frequently verbalized in statements such as the following: "If such a literature exists, someone would first have to convince me that the methodology is sound and that these people have anything of substance to say" or "Teaching is a mystical experience. No one really knows anything about teaching. Sometimes I have taught two sections of the same course, and one has gone extremely well, whereas the other has been a disaster. No one can really account for this."

Such resistance is understandable if faculty, whose profession it is to teach, have never become familiar with the literature on adult learning and motivation or teaching pedagogy. Based on my experience in workshops I have conducted for department chairs and faculty at more than sixty college campuses over the past three years, most faculty are not familiar with this literature.

To enhance teaching effectiveness, department chairs need to (1) recognize that they have both position and personal power to accomplish such change, (2) be familiar with some strategies for bringing about change, and (3) have a general sense of the range of issues related to teaching about which faculty should become knowledgeable. Power and its influence on others, how it can be used effectively and collaboratively in an academic department (Lucas, 1989b; Tucker, 1984), and how it can be increased is widely discussed in the literature (Conger, Kanungo, and Associates, 1988; Kouzes and Posner, 1987).

Specific Interventions for Improving Teaching

Following are specific interventions a chair can use to improve teaching.

1. *Make teaching effectiveness a high-priority goal of the department.* Discuss your plans for enhancing teaching with the dean. A basic principle of good leadership is that the person to whom you report should never be surprised by what is going on. Deans can find ways of supporting what you are doing and be open to discussing your plans if you keep them informed as you go. Find formal and informal opportunities for talking about teaching with your colleagues in the department. Ask faculty how their classes are going. Share with them, on an individual basis, some innovations you are attempting in your courses. Ask for their advice, and listen to it.

2. *Create a climate of trust and support so that visiting one another's classrooms is acceptable and nonthreatening.* We can learn a great deal about teaching from one another, yet teaching is considered to be such a private activity that we lose opportunities to learn because little formal structure exists in most departments to allow teachers to benefit from what others are doing. Teaching effectively, like using anger and conflict creatively, is a lifetime project. We can always improve; to maximize our improvement, we need feedback from others. Therefore, break down barriers that make teaching a solitary activity and invite a colleague to visit your class. Tell this person about the kind of feedback you would appreciate and establish certain guidelines. Ask what your colleague liked about your class. Positive feedback should always precede the negative. Be realistic. Ask only for as much feedback as you can accept and structure your questions accordingly. For example, what strategies were most successful in involving students in class discussion? Can you suggest one or two other approaches I could try? If negative comments are offered, do not defend yourself. If you become defensive when asking for feedback, it will be the last time that individual will respond to your request. Instead, paraphrase

what you have heard and ask for examples if feedback is not clear. If you feel the feedback has been useful, incorporate some of the suggestions made in your next class. If these work well, share this information with the colleague who made the recommendations.

3. *Require all applicants for faculty positions to make a presentation to faculty and students before receiving a faculty appointment.* Have students and faculty discuss and evaluate together the lecture or discussion. Such an evaluation will also be informative to faculty in terms of what students value.

4. *Reward good teaching.* Since money is not usually available for this purpose in most institutions, the rewards referred to are recognition and positive reinforcement. Tell colleagues when you have heard something good about their teaching. Colleges and universities are bureaucracies in which there exists a vacuum in terms of individual reward. Be imaginative! Find opportunities for recognizing the good work colleagues are doing in the classroom.

5. *Talk about the many aspects of teaching at department meetings or at workshops sponsored by your department.* Invite someone from your faculty development office to give a workshop on a selected topic. Have an occasional brown-bag lunch with faculty members, with the announced topic being, for example, sharing strategies on how to motivate students. (It might be good to invite some students, but do not attack them if they make negative comments about their classroom experiences.) Provide travel money for a faculty member to attend a workshop on teaching and have him or her share in considerable detail the workshop content and handouts with colleagues at a department meeting.

6. *Share your course syllabus.* Although such sharing may initially be met with a healthy skepticism, chairs who circulate course syllabi typically find that considerable learning occurs as faculty become more thoughtful about developing course outlines and preparing teaching materials (Trask, 1989).

7. *Provide feedback to department members by circulating an anonymous list of grade distributions,* each copy identi-

fying by name only the grades given by the one faculty member who receives the list. Introducing the topic of grade inflation or dealing with a colleague who prides him- or herself on giving 45 percent of the students D's and F's is admittedly fraught with difficulties. However, when faculty members have an opportunity to compare their grade distributions with others in the department, they often voluntarily make adjustments in a more realistic direction. At the very least, the basis for grading and colleague expectations can more easily become a topic for discussion at a department meeting.

8. *Begin a teaching committee.* Such a committee might be divided into subcommittees that deal with classroom instruction, curriculum, and peer evaluation. Faculty are sometimes more responsive to workshops on teaching planned by colleagues but clearly supported by the chair.

9. *Build a department library on teaching.* Such literature is becoming very rich and comprehensive. References are provided later in the chapter for books and articles that could be acquired gradually to provide a readily available resource for faculty on teaching and learning.

10. *Use student and colleague evaluations as feedback to celebrate good teaching.* When appropriate, develop a specific plan and follow-up on the plan to improve teaching techniques and approaches.

11. *Develop a mentoring system.* This strategy involves having two faculty members work together as a team of teacher and observer. Both of them interview approximately three students from one of their classes once a week during the semester. Interviews focus not on the teacher but on students and their ways of learning, how they read assignments and prepare for class, and the student-teacher interactions during class periods. The teacher and observer then meet for about one hour once a week to discuss the implications of these interviews with respect to how the course is taught. Faculty involved in such a program are usually extremely enthusiastic about the ways in which the mentoring process can benefit their teaching (Katz, 1985; Katz and Henry, 1988).

12. *Introduce classroom research techniques for evaluat-*

ing the effectiveness of teaching strategies and aiding under-standing of what is going on in the classroom. A variety of simple research tools can be used to discover what topics and approaches students are most enthusiastic about, what we were doing at the time in the semester when a number of students stopped attending class, the nature of student expec-tations, and what works and what does not work in the courses we teach.

13. *Send interested faculty to workshops on teaching and have them run a workshop when they return.*

How to Get Started

Faculty members would generally agree that they place a high value on teaching. But when was the last time we discussed it within the department? When did we last share with each other information about a class that went really well? When did we last ask a colleague for advice on how best to present a difficult concept? Does the topic of teaching ever come up at a department meeting?

Since the subject of what goes on in the classroom seems to be very private in many colleges, how does a chair introduce the topic of teaching effectiveness in the depart-ment? Being an effective leader requires that one take risks and be willing to fail. Obviously, not everything we try will work. One of the functions of leadership is to initiate the structure to make something happen. A chair has the power to set the agenda for department meetings. (Of course, once a preliminary agenda is developed, a chair also asks for addi-tional agenda items from faculty.) A chair can place instruc-tional development on the agenda. When this item comes up at a meeting, how does a chair handle the topic? A chair might say something like, "I placed this item on the agenda because I've been reading about some recent innovations in college teaching, things such as how one can get students more actively involved in the classroom, how to lead good discussions, how to teach critical thinking, how to maximize the learning of adult students. It occurs to me that we haven't talked about teaching in a long time, and yet we all value good teaching. I was wondering if two or three of you would be willing to share at a workshop for the rest of us some of the teaching strategies you have tried that really worked in getting students more involved in class. Jim, I've heard students talk about some of the small-group work (or experiential learning, or role play, or case studies) you have used in your classes. Would you be willing to share that approach with us? Thank you. I'd also like to have one or two other individuals share some ideas. Who else would be willing to do this?" During this department meeting, determine the date and time of the workshop and indicate your firm expectation that every member of the department will attend because teaching is an issue that is central to enhancing the quality of the undergraduate experience.

Be certain to include in the minutes of the department meeting the discussion and plans for a workshop on teaching. Write notes thanking those who volunteered to be presenters. As the date for the workshop approaches, send out a memo reminding the faculty of this event. Adopt an enthusiastic tone. Think through in advance what role you will play in the workshop. Will you introduce the discussion, chair a panel, take an active part in the discussion of teaching strategies that follows the formal presentation, or simply thank the presenters at the end of the workshop? Whatever you choose to do, be certain to ask what kind of follow-up faculty members want and line up a topic and presenters for another workshop that same semester. It is likely that faculty will find such discussions stimulating and informative and will welcome the opportunity to bring up issues related to the teaching process. Most will probably come away from these discussions with strategies they can use in their own classes.

Topics to Explore in Departmental Meetings

Once the subject of teaching is legitimized as a topic worthy of attention, there are many issues to be explored. Although some of these may have surfaced (and been treated in a cursory fashion) in connection with other subjects at department meetings, the topics listed below merit some consideration by faculty who are willing to make a commitment to instructional effectiveness. References are provided as sources of additional information on the topic.

1. What constitutes effective teaching? (Daloz, 1986; Ericksen, 1984; Lowman, 1984)
2. How do we motivate students? (Lucas, 1990; Katz and Henry, 1988)
3. How can we reinforce students' efforts and improvement without creating grade inflation? (Milton, Pollio, and Eison, 1986)
4. What makes a lecture good? (Eble, 1988; Lowman, 1984)
5. What are some alternatives to lecturing? What are some useful strategies for leading a discussion? (Frederick, 1989)
6. How can we involve students more actively in learning? (Wilkerson and Feletti, 1989)
7. How can the first day of class be used to create positive student norms and expectations for the rest of the semester? (Lucas, 1990)
8. What is collaborative learning, and how can it be used as an alternative to traditional classroom learning? (Bruffee, 1984)
9. How can our discipline be used to teach critical thinking? (Browne, 1986; Kurfiss, 1988, 1989)
10. How do students' levels of cognitive development affect what and how they learn, and what are the implications for teaching? (Perry, 1970, 1981)
11. What are departmental expectations for student performance? (Milton, Pollio, and Eison, 1986)
12. How can examinations be constructed so that they reflect the goals of a course? (Bloom, 1956; Bloom, Madaus, and Hastings, 1981)
13. What are some classroom factors related to increasing student retention? (National Institute of Education, 1984; Noel, Levitz, and Saluri, 1985; Noel and Levitz, 1986)

14. How can classroom management issues (for example, students who dominate discussions, are disruptive, or shy) be handled? (Eble, 1988; McKeachie, 1986)
15. How do we prevent cheating and plagiarism? (Center for Teaching Effectiveness, 1985)
16. How can we communicate clear-cut expectations to students? (Altman, 1989)
17. What are some of the better ways of handling students who come to class unprepared? (Eble, 1988; Lucas, 1990)
18. What are the essential ingredients in a course syllabus? (Mager, 1984; Wilkerson and McKnight, 1978)
19. How can student and colleague evaluations be used to improve teaching effectiveness? (Lucas, 1989a; Menges, this volume)
20. What is the purpose of feedback and its implications for grading and returning papers and exams? (Milton, Pollio, and Eison, 1986)
21. What are the different levels of educational goals tapped by various kinds of questions asked in class or on examinations? (Bloom, 1956; Bloom, Madaus, and Hastings, 1981)
22. How can large sections be taught most effectively? (Lewis, 1987; Weimer, 1987)
23. How can we deal with classes that vary markedly in terms of different student characteristics such as intelligence, prior knowledge, cognitive stage, and sex? (Belenky, Clinchy, Goldberger, and Tarule, 1986; McKeachie, 1986; Perry, 1970, 1981)
24. What special considerations and practices are useful in teaching classes in which there is cultural diversity? (Banks, 1988)
25. What classroom research techniques will provide information on the relationship between specific teaching techniques in an individual course and student learning? (Cross and Angelo, 1988)
26. How does one assess institutional, program, and instructional outcomes? (Gardiner, 1989)

27. How does one go about planning a new course, curriculum, or program? (Diamond, 1989)

Motivating Alienated Tenured Faculty

What motivates faculty? Faculty members are clearly among the most intelligent members of our society; probably most are in the top 5 percent of the population. Also, all faculty were once highly motivated. They had to be to overcome the series of hurdles involved in completing a graduate degree, particularly a Ph.D. How can they be motivated again?

The human resource development model suggests that when department goals are met by also achieving individual goals, motivation is greatest. But what are faculty members' goals? Faculty are most likely to be motivated when they feel they are part of an important ongoing enterprise—when they feel that they make a difference. We can all remember a time when we worked incredibly long hours each week because we felt that something we were doing was important and that we were making a significant contribution to something we believed in. For example, Apple's Macintosh computer development group wore sweatshirts on the front of which was printed the Macintosh insignia and on the back "90 hours a week and loving it" (Kouzes and Posner, 1987, p. 194). It also helps if we feel someone else appreciates what we are contributing. The task of the transformational leader is to challenge a system that maintains that a chair has no power to motivate faculty and to empower others to carry out their own good ideas, "inspiring others to excel, giving individual consideration to others, and stimulating people to think in new ways" (Kouzes and Posner, 1987, p. 281).

In my survey of department chairs, motivating alienated tenured faculty members is a task that department chairs most frequently feel they have not completed successfully. How do faculty members become alienated, and what can we do about it? Most of us came into higher education with a dream. That dream may have focused on being part of a community of scholars from whom we would receive intellectual stimulation and emotional support in our discipline. Perhaps we felt we would do that definitive research study and share our findings with others. Or our dream may have emphasized passing on the torch to the next generation of scholars. We might have dreamed that students would listen attentively to every word we said and be inspired by us. However, once we joined a college or university—slowly for some, quickly for others—we began to separate the realities of academe from the dream with which we started.

Many new faculty members walk into a classroom for the first time with a role model of a favorite professor in mind and use those teaching strategies used by their most-admired former teacher. But before too many semesters pass, some discover that their teaching is less than satisfying. Moreover, it is humiliating to admit to having problems reaching students. Since almost everyone seems to take it for granted that getting a Ph.D. prepares one for the demands of teaching, there seems to be nowhere to turn for help. Years go by, and rationalizations develop to protect self-esteem. A typical rationalization is, "Although I am well qualified and an excellent teacher, students these days are not intelligent enough, not well motivated, or don't have the skills to benefit from what I have to offer."

Other faculty become alienated later. After holding a place of esteem in their departments, there comes a time when their opinions and advice seem to be ignored. Or, after occupying a position of prestige, they see others assume leadership roles in a department. This is painful, and faculty members may show by their behavior that they are displeased and may make their lack of support clear by indicating they are not committed to particular projects enthusiastically espoused by others in the department. As time goes on, their displeasure is felt by other members of the department, and these disgruntled members begin to be ignored. They and their colleagues become adversaries, and each believes that it is too late to repair the rift. The alienated faculty members may look for some outside activities, which sometimes may be prestigious consulting work but often is something mundane, such as painting apartments, opening a motorcycle shop, or starting a business. Engaging in such activities often has symbolic value: "If I am not appreciated by my colleagues, I can at least do other things to increase my income or help me gain some satisfaction."

How can a department chair motivate such alienated faculty members? A successful approach often involves something as simple as demonstrating some human caring. There are teachers in the department who have not said more than "Hello" to another member of the department for years. A chair can make a point of greeting such faculty members warmly, asking how things are going, discussing some topic of general or academic interest, asking their opinions or advice about something, even occasionally inviting them to lunch.

At some point one might say something like, "You haven't been to a department meeting in a long time. I remember when I used to look forward to hearing your point of view on issues we discussed. What keeps you away these days?" If this question releases a tirade, do not try to correct the perceptions. Do some active listening and nonjudgmental summarization of what you hear. When some of the emotion is spent and the bitterness aired, you might say, "I think I have a better understanding of how you feel. But we'd really like to have you back as part of the team." No agreement may be reached on that occasion, but you will have other opportunities, and the faculty member will have time to think about what you have said. Another approach is to ask alienated faculty members to attend a meeting to give a report on a relevant topic, one that you know they are knowledgeable about. When they do, be sure to let them know that you appreciate their effort. Or, if you know of an area in which they have some particular expertise, find a way of using this knowledge in the department. Often, alienated faculty members would like to find a way back into the mainstream but may be too proud, or too concerned about possible rejection, to try to do so on their own.

Moreover, there are some departments in which a

destructive climate has been permitted to exist for years. This may be because one autocratic or ineffective individual has held the position of chair for a long time. Or it may be that negative behaviors that have become deeply embedded have not been confronted by new chairs. Effective department chairs foster collaboration, create win-win resolutions, and promote integrative solutions to problems. Chairs who are strong leaders let faculty know their input is personally valued. Since financial resources are often limited in higher education—and, indeed, are not a powerful source of motivation—chairs need to generate alternative "currencies" by identifying what others want. Visibility and recognition, often through sharing credit for any project's success, are the most important currencies available to department chairs (Kanter, 1983).

Orienting New Faculty

Since it is so difficult to reverse the process of alienation, preventing it might be a better approach. Estimates of the number of new faculty that will be hired in postsecondary education between now and the year 2004 are as high as 335,000. However, many of these new faculty members will be integrated into departments in which faculty have lost their excitement about teaching and department chairs feel powerless to create any meaningful change. Therefore, it is important to allocate the necessary resources to support new faculty members in developing their teaching skills and discovering how students learn and are motivated.

One way to do this is to take the time to provide material on learning and motivation and on teaching pedagogy. Their classes should be observed by colleagues or chairs, and feedback should be given so that successes can be celebrated and plans can be developed to address ineffective approaches. Alternatively, a videotape can be made of a new faculty member teaching a class. The teacher can then use a behavioral check list, such as TABS (Teaching Analysis by Students), to identify the strategies they are using that are effective and those that are not. Another useful way for faculty to develop a new understanding of what is happening in the classroom is through the mentoring system proposed by Katz and Henry (1988). A new faculty member might even be paired up with a burned-out faculty member who has good teaching skills. Such an arrangement can revitalize the senior faculty member, who may be able to view the complexity of teaching from a new perspective.

Working with Burned-Out Faculty

For faculty members who have been teaching the same courses (particularly introductory or service courses) and taking the same committee assignments for a number of years, faculty life can become repetitious and dull, or as Eble (1988, p. 190) puts it, "Too many students, too many papers, too much going over the same ground . . . the pressures, the details, the small audience response." Professional growth and change are the most useful prescriptions for such individuals—a challenging assignment, a new course, a different responsibility, or a new activity. Tucker (1984) lists dozens of possibilities, including short visits to neighboring colleges or universities, special assignments in administrative posts on campus, teaming with a colleague to write a journal article, taking a continuing education course, or visiting classes conducted by colleagues.

A chair can help prevent burnout and provide overall faculty motivation by creating a departmental climate of commitment and enthusiasm. Again, when dealing with burned-out faculty, as with alienated faculty, it is important to take the time to talk with them individually. Be a receptive listener. Discuss the dream that brought them into higher education and what happened to that dream. Find out how they think about what they are doing, what they consider personal successes or failures. Often, burned-out faculty denigrate the value of what they are doing. It is useful when someone they respect offers a more realistic and positive perspective about their accomplishments. Help them identify some new activities that would make teaching more interesting and satisfying. Developing new long- and short-term goals for professional development is useful. It is particularly valuable to identify some activity that provides an immediate opportunity for accomplishment, thereby providing these teachers with a reason for optimism.

Improving the Performance of Poor Teachers

This chapter began by offering some suggestions on creating a departmental climate that (1) values and recognizes quality teaching, (2) stimulates faculty to investigate how the content of a discipline can be taught rather than just what material should be covered, and (3) explores how students learn and are motivated. Changing the climate is most likely to create the significant behavior change that will improve departmental teaching over the long term, but this takes time. For the chair who faces an immediate problem of dealing with a poor teacher, some additional recommendations are offered. First, timing is important. A generally good principle is to intervene as quickly as possible once it is recognized that a faculty member is having problems. Dysfunctional behavior tends to be repeated when a teacher does not recognize that there are alternative ways of teaching and interacting with students and then rationalizes why teaching methods did not work as they should have, for example, "How I teach would be effective if students were motivated (or had the necessary level of academic skills, or would do their assignments, and so on)."

If the individual is not yet tenured, intervention is easier, because most institutions expect that nontenured faculty will be evaluated by a colleague or chair on a regular basis. However, if the ineffective teacher already has tenure, gaining entrance to the faculty member's classroom becomes difficult. Since people are not generally terminated because they are poor teachers, the chair's goal should be to conduct a formative evaluation—that is, an assessment for the purpose of instructional improvement. If trust has been established in the department, this process is easier. An effective approach is to look at poor teaching as a problem to be solved rather than as a failing to be criticized. When student evaluations are low or students complain to the chair about a faculty member's teaching, something is going wrong. If a problem-solving approach is used, most individuals will not object to a visit by the chair or a member of a teaching committee. In some unionized institutions in which a chair is a member of the bargaining unit, such a visit may be unheard of. Sometimes it helps to have one or two senior faculty invite the chair to visit their classrooms so that a visit to an ineffective teacher's class is not seen as unusual.

Once a classroom observation has been completed, the following procedures for conducting a feedback interview are recommended by Lucas (1989a):

1. Create a supportive climate characterized by trust.
2. Emphasize the positive performance that was observed.
3. Provide corroborative evidence of areas that require improvement (this might come from student evaluations).
4. Develop the faculty member's ownership of both problem definition and possible solutions.
5. Agree on strategies for improvement.
6. Provide for further contacts to discuss progress.

Recommendations for Effective Chair Leadership

The department chair can be the most effective agent of change in a college or university, but to be effective, chairs require empowerment, knowledge, and leadership skills. Topics that should be covered in leadership skills training programs follow (Lucas, 1986a, 1986b, 1989b; Tucker, 1984):

- Roles and responsibilities of a department chair
- Effective interpersonal communication
- How to motivate faculty
- How to resolve conflict through problem solving
- Performance counseling
- Team leadership and effective group behavior

- Faculty development
- Decision making
- How to bring about change
- Managing conflicts.

Chairs need an organizational climate that both values and supports leadership development. The impact of an increasing emphasis on accountability in higher education seems to have fallen on department chairs, and departmental expectations for accountability cannot be addressed without administrative recognition of the change in the role of the chair and administrative support for such responsibility.

Finally, chairs need the empowerment of support from deans and vice-presidents. If faculty are permitted to bring problems directly to a dean and bypass the chair, the authority of a chair is undermined. When any part of the distribution of concrete rewards is taken away from chairs, the power of the chair to motivate faculty is diminished. If chairs feel they will receive no support from a dean when it is necessary to confront a faculty member who is not performing in a responsible manner, chairs will, with justification, feel powerless. Chairs will also be convinced that there is nothing they can do to enforce accountability in departments. In such cases, the college or university loses the opportunity to improve teaching.

The role conflict of being both faculty member and administrator, the impact of increasing institutional emphasis on accountability, the overwhelming amount of paperwork, the problems of working with difficult colleagues, the need to motivate faculty, and the constant demands of their own scholarship make the job of chairing a department an extremely challenging task. Given this, it is crucial that chairs continue their own professional development.

It is important to set priorities. You might begin by reviewing the way you spend your time. You can monitor your activities for a week and then ask, "Considering my own priorities and values, am I allocating my time the way I want to?" By implication, if you want to devote time to advance your own scholarship, make that time an essential part of your day. The most important point of this exercise is to regain a sense of control over your own life. Knowing we are in charge of our lives, versus feeling that the demands of others are so heavy we have no control over our lives, is crucial for good physical and psychological health. Ways to achieve this goal include being aware of and changing negative irrational thoughts, developing a good support network, making physical exercise and relaxation an integral part of your daily regimen, building in some private time for yourself each day, and deliberately savoring accomplishments (even small ones). Beech, Burns, and Sheffield (1982) and Burns (1980) provide helpful ideas for such practical approaches.

Leadership is a challenge. We must see things as they might be and thereby create a vision of the future. We need to inspire others by sharing this vision and empowering them to realize it. We can make our departments places in which people share a sense of excitement and know they make a difference. Chairs are in a singular position to make these things happen. Such behaviors are also what distinguish leaders from managers. Will chairs serve out their terms defending the view that there is nothing they can do to improve teaching in the department? The challenge is for chairs to realize that they can create a climate that values teaching and inspires colleagues to discover more about how students learn and how faculty can become effective teachers.

References

Altman, H. "Syllabus Shares 'What the Teacher Wants.' " *The Teaching Professor,* 1989, *3* (5), 1.

Banks, J. A. *Multiethnic Education: Theory and Practice.* (2nd ed.) Newton, Mass.: Allyn & Bacon, 1988.

Beech, H. R., Burns, L. E., and Sheffield, B. F. *A Behavioral Approach to the Management of Stress: A Practical Guide to Techniques.* New York: Wiley, 1982.

Belenky, M., Clinchy, B., Goldberger, N., and Tarule, J. *Women's Ways of Knowing.* New York: Basic Books, 1986.

Bennett, W. "To Reclaim a Legacy." *Chronicle of Higher Education,* Nov. 28, 1984, pp. 16–21.

Bennett, W. "Address Given at the Harvard University Three Hundred and Fiftieth Anniversary Celebration." *Chronicle of Higher Education,* Oct. 15, 1986, pp. 27–30.

Bloom, A. *The Closing of the American Mind.* New York: Simon & Schuster, 1987.

Bloom, B. S. (ed.). *Taxonomy of Educational Objectives: Cognitive Domain.* New York: Longmans, Green, 1956.

Bloom, B. S., Madaus, G. F., and Hastings, J. T. *Evaluation to Improve Learning.* New York: McGraw-Hill, 1981.

Boyer, E. L. *College: The Undergraduate Experience in America.* New York: Harper & Row, 1987.

Browne, N. *Asking the Right Questions: A Guide to Critical Thinking.* Englewood Cliffs, N.J.: Prentice-Hall, 1986.

Bruffee, K. A. "Collaborative Learning and the 'Conversation of Mankind.' " *College English,* 1984, *46* (7), 635–652.

Center for Teaching Effectiveness. *Teachers Can Make a Difference. (Sourcebook for New Faculty).* Austin: Center for Teaching Effectiveness, University of Texas at Austin, 1985.

Clark, B. R. *The Academic Life: Small Worlds, Different Worlds.* Princeton, N.J.: Princeton University Press, 1987.

Conger, J. A., Kanungo, R. N., and Associates. *Charismatic Leadership.* San Francisco: Jossey-Bass, 1988.

Cross, K. P. "Not Can but Will College Teaching Be Improved?" In J. A. Centra (ed.), *Renewing and Evaluating Teaching.* New Directions for Higher Education, no. 17. San Francisco: Jossey-Bass, 1977.

Cross, K. P., and Angelo, T. A. *Classroom Assessment Techniques: A Handbook for Faculty.* Ann Arbor: Board of Regents, National Center for Research to Improve Postsecondary Teaching and Learning, University of Michigan, 1988.

Daloz, L. A. *Effective Teaching and Mentoring: Realizing the Transformational Power of Adult Learning Experiences.* San Francisco: Jossey-Bass, 1986.

Diamond, R. M. *Designing and Improving Courses and Curricula in Higher Education: A Systematic Approach.* San Francisco: Jossey-Bass, 1989.

Eble, K. E. *The Aims of College Teaching.* San Francisco: Jossey-Bass, 1983.

Eble, K. E. *The Craft of Teaching.* (2nd ed.) San Francisco: Jossey-Bass, 1988.

Edgerton, R. "Melange." *Chronicle of Higher Education,* Apr. 20, 1988, p. B2.

Ericksen, S. C. *The Essence of Good Teaching: Helping Students Learn and Remember What They Learn.* San Francisco: Jossey-Bass, 1984.

Frederick, P. J. "Involving Students More Actively in the Classroom." In A. F. Lucas (ed.), *The Department Chairperson's Role in Enhancing College Teaching.* New Directions for Teaching and Learning, no. 37. San Francisco: Jossey-Bass, 1989.

Gardiner, L. *Planning for Assessment: Mission Statements, Goals, and Objectives.* Trenton: Office of Learning Assessment, New Jersey Department of Higher Education, 1989.

Hirsch, E. D., Jr. *Cultural Literacy.* Boston: Houghton Mifflin, 1987.

Kanter, R. M. *The Change Masters.* New York: Simon & Schuster, 1983.

Katz, J. *Teaching as Though Students Mattered.* New Directions for Teaching and Learning, no. 21. San Francisco: Jossey-Bass, 1985.

Katz, J., and Henry, M. *Turning Professors into Teachers.* New York: ACE/Macmillan, 1988.

Kouzes, J. M., and Posner, B. Z. *The Leadership Challenge: How to Get Extraordinary Things Done in Organizations.* San Francisco: Jossey-Bass, 1987.

Kurfiss, J. G. *Critical Thinking: Theory, Research, Practice, and Possibilities.* Washington, D.C.: Association for the Study of Higher Education, 1988.

Kurfiss, J. G. "Helping Faculty Foster Students' Critical Thinking in the Disciplines." In A. F. Lucas (ed.), *The Department Chairperson's Role in Enhancing College Teaching.* New Directions for Teaching and Learning, no. 37. San Francisco: Jossey-Bass, 1989.

Lewis, K. *Taming the Pedagogical Monster: A Handbook for Large Class Instructors.* Austin: Center for Teaching Effectiveness, University of Texas at Austin, 1987.

Lowman, J. *Mastering the Techniques of Teaching.* San Francisco: Jossey-Bass, 1984.

Lucas, A. "Academic Chair Training: The Why and the How of It." In M. Svinicki (ed.), *To Improve the Academy.* Stillwater, Okla.: New Forums Press, 1986a.

Lucas, A. "Effective Department Chair Training on a Low-Cost Budget." *Journal of Staff, Program, and Organization Development,* 1986b, *4* (4), 33–36.

Lucas, A. "Using Student Evaluations as a Tool to Improve Faculty Teaching: Conducting the Feedback Interview." In *Proceedings* of the Sixth Annual Conference on National Issues in Higher Education, *Academic Chairpersons: Evaluating Faculty, Students, and Programs,* Kansas State University, Manhattan, Kansas, Feb. 1989a.

Lucas, A. F. (ed.). *The Department Chairperson's Role in Enhancing College Teaching.* New Directions for Teaching and Learning, no. 37. San Francisco: Jossey-Bass, 1989b.

Lucas, A. "Motivating Students." In M. Svinicki (ed.), *The Changing Face of College Teaching.* New Directions for Teaching and Learning, no. 42. San Francisco: Jossey-Bass, 1990.

McKeachie, W. J. *Teaching Tips: A Guidebook for the Beginning College Teacher.* (8th ed.) Lexington, Mass.: Heath, 1986.

McMillen, L. "Job-Related Tension and Anxiety Taking a Toll Among Employees in Academe's Stress Factories." *Chronicle of Higher Education,* Feb. 4, 1987, p. 1.

Mager, R. F. *Preparing Instructional Objectives.* (2nd ed.) Belmont, Calif.: Pitman, 1984.

Mangan, K. S. "Research Universities Urged to Upgrade Status of Teaching." *Chronicle of Higher Education,* Nov. 4, 1987, p. A19.

Milton, O., Pollio, H. R., and Eison, J. A. *Making Sense of College Grades.* San Francisco: Jossey-Bass, 1986.

National Institute of Education. *Involvement in Learning: Realizing the Potential of American Higher Education.* Final report of the Study Group on Conditions of Excellence in American Higher Education. Washington, D.C.: National Institute of Education, 1984.

Newman, F. *Higher Education and the American Resurgence.* Princeton, N.J.: Princeton University Press, 1985.

Noel, L., and Levitz, R. "Student Retention Strategies and Practices." Unpublished manuscript prepared for Fund for the Improvement of Collegiate Education, State of New Jersey Department of Higher Education, 1986.

Noel, L., Levitz, R., Saluri, D., and Associates (eds.). *Increasing Student Retention.* San Francisco: Jossey-Bass, 1985.

Perry, W. G., Jr. *Forms of Intellectual and Ethical Development in the College Years: A Scheme.* New York: Holt, Rinehart & Winston, 1970.

Perry, W. G., Jr. "Cognitive and Ethical Growth: The Making of Meaning." In A. W. Chickering and Associates (eds.), *The Modern American College: Responding to the New Realities of Diverse Students and a Changing Society.* San Francisco: Jossey-Bass, 1981.

Rice, R. E., and Austin, A. *Community, Commitment, and Congruence: A Different Kind of Excellence. A Preliminary Report on the Future of the Academic Workplace in Liberal Arts Colleges.* Washington, D.C.: Council of Independent Colleges, 1987.

Roueche, J. E., Baker, G. A., and Roueche, S. D. *College Responses to Low-Achieving Students: A National Study.* San Diego, Calif.: Harcourt Brace Jovanovich, 1984.

Seldin, P. *Changing Practices in Faculty Evaluation.* San Francisco: Jossey-Bass, 1985.

Seldin, P. (ed.). *Coping with Faculty Stress.* New Directions for Teaching and Learning, no. 29. San Francisco: Jossey-Bass, 1987.

Trask, K. A. "The Chairperson and Teaching." In A. F. Lucas (ed.), *The Department Chairperson's Role in Enhancing College Teaching.* New Directions for Teaching and Learning, no. 37. San Francisco: Jossey-Bass, 1989.

Tucker, A. *Chairing the Academic Department.* New York: Macmillan, 1984.

Weimer, M. G. (ed.). *Teaching Large Classes Well.* New Directions for Teaching and Learning, no. 32. San Francisco: Jossey-Bass, 1987.

Wilkerson, L., and Feletti, G. "Problem-Based Learning: One Approach to Increasing Student Participation." In A. F. Lucas (ed.), *The Department Chairperson's Role in Enhancing College Teaching*. New Directions for Teaching and Learning, no. 37. San Francisco: Jossey-Bass, 1989.

Wilkerson, L., and McKnight, R. T. "Writing a Course Syllabus: A Self-Study Packet for College Teachers." Unpublished manuscript, New Pathway Project, Harvard Medical School, Cambridge, Mass., 1978.

CHAPTER 5

Assessing
Teaching Effectiveness
William E. Cashin

Almost every institution of higher education states somewhere that the primary purpose of the institution is teaching. Commitment to teaching certainly varies from institution to institution, but every college or university assesses teaching in some way. Increasingly, higher education's various publics—students, parents, legislators, and others—are insisting that teaching be assessed seriously and substantively. The time has come for higher education to put its actions where its rhetoric is. My belief is that most colleges and universities are willing to do this. The problem is how.

This chapter describes the kinds of data that have been used to assess teaching effectiveness. Although the focus of this book is on improving teaching rather than evaluating it for personnel decisions, the two are necessarily bound together, not only in the minds of the faculty but in effective practice. Perhaps the most important action an academic administrator can take to improve teaching is to assess it accurately and to reward effective teachers. To tell faculty that the institution values teaching and wants them to improve their teaching when it really rewards research is not a credible message. "Improvement" does not necessarily mean that one's teaching is deficient: it simply means that it is not perfect. A teacher moving from B-level to A-level teaching is improving, but he or she is improving an already strong performance.

True, one can take a simpler approach to teaching improvement: any data that provide a clue to the teacher about how he or she might improve will serve. Let the teacher decide. Most academics find a better organized approach more useful. Therefore, this chapter will discuss data that are used to evaluate teaching for personnel decisions in addition to data used for improvement. First, this will give the reader a more complete frame of reference. Second, whenever you, as an administrator, talk about assessing teaching, even if you are thinking solely about improvement, your faculty will also be thinking about evaluation for personnel decisions.

There is considerable research on student ratings. But for most of the other sources of data, there is only experience—or in some cases opinion—to serve as a guide. (I have tried to keep the references to a minimum, citing only a few secondary summaries of the literature. These should give the interested academic administrator a starting place if he or she wants to read more on any topic.)

In this chapter, I first outline the kinds of information most often discussed when talking about assessing college teaching. Then I examine student ratings, the most frequently used kind of data. Finally, I talk about some less frequently used—but potentially effective—kinds of data: course materials, classroom observations, and videotapes. In each section, I will make recommendations about what academic administrators can do to gather accurate data about teaching effectiveness—the first step in improving teaching. In the next chapter, Menges will discuss ways to use some of these data for improvement. The reader is cautioned, however, that the degree of confidence you can place in these recommendations varies. Some recommendations are based on a considerable body of systematic research, and we therefore can have considerable confidence in them. Other recommendations come from a growing consensus based on experience but they have not been tested. Finally, some are primarily my opinion, and so that fact should be taken into account.

Sources of Data Used to Assess Teaching

In a study published in 1977 Centra (1979) surveyed 453 department heads, asking them to rate the current use and importance of fifteen sources of data in evaluating teaching for personnel decisions. In the previous year Centra (1979) had published a study on faculty development. The only additional sources of data included in his first study related to using teaching experts—that is, instructional consultants and master teachers. Centra's 1977 survey not only provides a useful list of possible sources of data but also summarizes most of the sources that had been used in previous and subsequent research. For example, Seldin (1984) used essentially the same list in his 1978 and 1983 surveys of liberal arts colleges. Listed below are the fifteen sources that Centra used, in their order of importance based on the ratings of all 453 department heads.

1st	Chairman evaluation
2nd (tied)	Colleagues' opinions
2nd (tied)	Systematic student ratings
4th	Committee evaluation
5th	Informal student opinions
6th	Dean evaluation
7th	Content of course syllabi and examinations
8th	Popularity of elective courses (for example, enrollment)
9th	Self-evaluation or report
10th	Teaching improvement activities
11th	Student examination performance
12th	Colleague ratings based on classroom visits
13th	Alumni opinions or ratings
14th	Long-term follow up of student performance
15th	Videotape of classroom teaching

The above list has the obvious advantage of outlining what kinds of data have been used by colleges and universities to evaluate teaching. A second reading, however, may suggest some problems. It seems to me that at least four of these

sources—chairman evaluation, colleagues' opinions, committee evaluation, and dean evaluation—are not sources of data
but opinions of people who evaluate—namely, the evaluators.
How does a chairman know whether a faculty member is an
effective teacher? Does he or she depend on the complaints of
a few students, gossip in the faculty lounge, or comments
overheard through an open classroom door? Or does the chairperson use systematic student ratings, surveys of the department faculty, and classroom observation? I suggest that most
of the data actually used by the chair, colleagues, committees,
or the dean come from other sources on the list. Some writers
have suggested that most of our judgments are really based on
secondhand student opinion.

Others ask the question "Is the list complete?" Arreola
(1986) argues—persuasively I think—that a total definition of
teaching should include three broad dimensions: (1) content
expertise, (2) instructional delivery skills and characteristics,
and (3) instructional design skills. Most of the data on Centra's list are mainly concerned with Arreola's second dimension—different aspects of classroom instruction.

Building on Arreola's and Centra's work, I suggest that
college teaching involves the seven different aspects listed
below. Each is followed by one or more examples (see Cashin,
1989, for a more complete discussion):

1. Mastery of subject matter: degrees, certificates or licenses
2. Curriculum development: course revisions, new courses
3. Course design: syllabi, handouts
4. Delivery of instruction: student ratings, videotapes
5. Assessment of instruction: graded exams, projects, or
    papers
6. Availability to students: office hours
7. Administrative requirements: turning in book orders, pro-
    bation notices, grades.

If this is a more accurate list of the various aspects of college
teaching, there are some implicit problems for U.S. higher
education. Many believe, and I share the belief, that student

ratings are the only primary data that are systematically gathered at many colleges and universities. Most student rating forms are mainly concerned with delivery of instruction. Some forms may also provide information on the assessment of instruction and the instructor's availability to students. Nevertheless, at best these ratings usually cover only three of the seven aspects or areas. The discussion that follows assumes that in the past, evaluation practice has focused on the delivery and assessment of instruction and has often ignored other significant aspects of teaching. Such practice works against truly improving teaching.

Recommendation 1: Use multiple sources of data about a faculty member's teaching if you are serious about improving teaching.

Student Ratings of Teaching

There are probably more studies of student ratings (over 1,300) than of all of the other data used to evaluate faculty teaching, research, and service combined. Many student rating variables have been the subject of several studies, which reveal discernible trends. Reviewers of this literature generally conclude that student ratings are reliable, valid, and relatively free from bias. Student rating data provide one useful source of information to improve teaching. The following recommendations are based on the student rating research (see Marsh, 1984, and Cashin, 1988a, for reviews) unless otherwise noted.

Recommendation 2: Use student rating data as one source of data about effective teaching. Student ratings correlate reasonably well with measures of student learning, and with the ratings of administrators, faculty colleagues, instructor self-ratings, alumni ratings, and the ratings of trained observers.

Recommendation 3: To obtain reliable student rating data, collect data from at least ten raters.

Recommendation 4: To obtain representative student rating data, collect data from at least two-thirds of the class. (This is based on experience rather than research.)

Recommendation 5: To generalize from student rating data to an instructor's overall teaching effectiveness, use data from two or more different classes over three or more different terms.

Recommendation 6: Do not give undue weight to the following: the instructor's age, sex, teaching experience, personality, or research productivity; the student's age, sex, grade level, grade-point average, or personality; or the class size or time of day when taught. These items show little or no correlation with student ratings. It is not necessary to develop comparative data to control for them in your student rating system or to give them special consideration when interpreting student ratings. The exception is this: in specific cases the above factors should be considered if the instructor provides evidence for their influence in his or her self-report data or if you or others have such evidence.

Recommendation 7: Take into consideration the students' motivation level when interpreting student rating data. The research shows clearly that students who want to take the course, who have a strong prior interest in the subject matter, or, to a lesser extent, who elect the course rather than taking it because it was required tend to give higher ratings. Courses such as these are probably easier to teach effectively, which should be taken into account when reviewing the ratings.

Recommendation 8: Decide how you will treat student ratings from different academic fields. There is increasing evidence that different academic fields are rated differently. What is not clear is why. For example, more quantitative courses, such as mathematics, tend to receive lower ratings. If you think this is because these courses are more difficult to teach, then you should take that into consideration; if you think that they are more poorly taught, then you should not.

Regarding Recommendations 7 and 8, consider as an example a psychology instructor who receives somewhat lower ratings in the statistics course she teaches than for her abnormal psychology course. Should you recommend that she work to improve the statistics course first, or are the lower ratings because the course is heavily quantitative? Perhaps she would be better advised to direct her improvement efforts toward the abnormal psychology course, which is an elective and so generally should receive higher ratings.

Although there are a few studies related to the following recommendations regarding student ratings, these recommendations are based more on experience than on research.

Recommendation 9: Develop procedures that clearly differentiate the purpose—personnel decisions or improvement—of the ratings. Standardizing procedures helps clarify what data are being collected for what purpose(s) and so yields better data.

When collecting student rating data for personnel decisions, generally accepted practice recommends the following guidelines:

1. The instructor may hand out the materials and read the standardized instructions but should leave the room while students complete the ratings. The ratings should be collected by a neutral party.
2. The institution should develop standardized instructions that include the purpose(s) that the data will be used for and who will receive what information when. For example, will the instructor receive students' handwritten comments? In my opinion it is too costly and time consuming to have students' comments typed. However, students should be told that the instructor will be given their handwritten comments; thus they can print or leave open-ended questions blank if they are concerned about confidentiality and possible retaliation. Some institutions print the open-ended questions on a separate sheet of paper and give it to students beforehand. This way students can take the questions home and type their responses if they wish.
3. Avoid administering the ratings on the last day of class or on the day of the final exam. In my opinion, the second to the last week of the term is a good time to obtain ratings. Students have an overall view of the course by this time but are not overly concerned about the final exam, turning in assignments, or the like.

4. The data should be taken to a predetermined location—often where they are scored—and should not be available to the instructor until the grades are turned in.
5. The standardized instructions should clearly state why the data are being collected and what the data will be used for. A few studies suggest that students will give higher ratings if the ratings are to be used for personnel decisions. Unless the instructions are clear about the purpose(s) of the ratings, there may be different results depending on what students guess is the purpose.
6. Do not require students to sign the ratings. Studies suggest that this will inflate the ratings.

When collecting student rating data for teaching improvement purposes, instructors are usually given wide latitude. Typically, the instructor gives and collects the ratings, which often consist of relatively few items. Such ratings include a few quantitative items: (1) Overall, how would you rate this instructor's teaching? (2) Overall, how would you rate this course? and (3) Overall, how much have you learned? Also included are a couple of open-ended questions: (1) Describe those things about the course that you find helpful, and (2) What suggestions do you have about how the course might be improved? These ratings should be collected after the first few weeks of the course so that there is time for the instructor to implement some of the students' suggestions. The instructor decides how the data will be used. Students usually like to give feedback early in the term, when it can do them some good. Instructors should be sure to follow up on at least some of the students' suggestions, or the students will conclude that the rating process was a waste of their time.

The kind of student rating data most often used for improvement are data that were collected for evaluation, because these are the kind of data most often available. The following recommendations concern how you can make your evaluation data also useful for improvement. These recommendations are based primarily on experience rather than research.

Recommendation 10: Develop a student rating system that is flexible. Instructional goals vary widely from course to course; your student rating system needs to accommodate this diversity. Using a standard form with a fixed set of questions implies that every instructor in every course should do all the things listed, which is rarely the case.

Recommendation 11: Provide comparative data, preferably for all the items. Without comparative data it is not possible to meaningfully interpret student rating data. For example, consider the example of the psychology instructor discussed above. If the instructor received ratings of 3 (on a five-point scale) on overall teaching effectiveness for both courses, would you conclude that her teaching was satisfactory? What would you conclude if you were told that a rating of 3 on this item was in the twentieth percentile? (That is, that 80 percent of instructors are rated higher than 3.) For the following two items—(1) seemed enthusiastic about the subject matter, and (2) explained the reasons for criticisms of students' academic performance—what would you advise her to work on for improvement if her two lowest ratings were on these two items, which were both rated 3.8? Would your advice change if you found out that a rating of 3.8 is at the sixteenth percentile for item 1 and at the eighty-fourth percentile for item 2? Comparative data are necessary if you are to make sense out of individual student rating items.

Recommendation 12: Provide controls for bias. Research evidence supports instituting some kind of control for student motivation. Some studies also reveal significant differences among course levels—that is, courses for freshmen, graduate students, and so on. These differences should be controlled for. You should also decide whether or not you are going to control for academic field. The way most campuses institute these controls is to develop separate tables for each variable— for example, one table for freshman classes, one for sophomore classes, and so on.

Recommendation 13: Develop a system that is diagnostic. When using student rating data to improve teaching, the more diagnostic the system is, the more useful it will be. This means that the items included on the form should be descriptive of specific, concrete teaching behaviors. The items should require as little inference as possible on the part of the student rater and little interpretation on the part of the instructor. For example, "The instructor provided an outline for each class, either on the chalkboard, a transparency, or in the syllabus or handout" is more diagnostic than an item such as "The instructor gave clear presentations." The drawback of such specific items is that there must be many items on the form to cover all major areas. The "cafeteria" approach—in which the instructor selects items from a large array—solves this problem particularly well. Since most faculty would be doing well to improve one course per term, I recommend that a long diagnostic form be used only for one course per term—for the course the instructor wishes to focus on for improvement. If student rating data are needed for other purposes, such as for personnel decisions, then a very short form with two to five summary-type items should be used.

Recommendation 14: Develop a system that is interpretable. Although educational measurement necessarily involves numbers, it is not necessary to report every single number. Ask yourself what use the teacher will make of any given bit of data. Also, I would suggest that reporting computations beyond the first decimal place is unnecessary and misleading, implying a level of precision rarely present. One major misuse of student ratings is overinterpretation of the data. Even reporting data to only the first decimal place yields 41 points, ranging from 1.0 to 5.0. Most student rating data are not this precise. Using frequency distributions—what number or percent of the students rated the item 1 or 2 and so on—is more understandable to most faculty than calculating a standard deviation for each item. Combining the data into five or perhaps ten categories and using descriptive words like *high* and so forth is more understandable and more realistically reflects the level of accuracy of the data.

Course Materials

Although student ratings are the most widely used—and certainly the most researched—source of data used to systematically improve teaching, there are other potentially helpful sources of data. Increasingly, course materials are being suggested in the literature as a data source (Centra, 1979; Seldin, 1980, 1984; Miller, 1987).

Recommendation 15: Use a variety of course materials when assessing an instructor's teaching effectiveness. Course materials should include not just the syllabus—or even just detailed course objectives—but also handouts, exams (including computer-analyzed results of multiple-choice tests, graded examples of essay tests, or papers and projects), and even lecture notes. Such materials provide evidence related to several aspects of teaching: course design, curriculum development, and mastery of the subject matter as well as assessment of instruction. Unlike student ratings, which require a special effort to collect, much or all of these materials are readily available.

Recommendation 16: Use the objectives of the course as the primary context for suggestions on how to improve course presentation. Ask to what extent the design of the course, the instruction itself, the testing structure, and so on help students achieve the objectives of the course. This, of course, presumes that the course objectives are clear to the instructor and have been explicitly stated to students. If such is not the case, perhaps the single best action the instructor can take to improve teaching the course may be to establish and state course objectives. For more detailed suggestions about what to consider when using course materials, see Braskamp, Brandenburg, and Ory (1984).

Although instructional consultants have long been using course objectives when working with individual instructors, the literature is just beginning to treat this topic systematically. One example is the work being done at the University of Michigan's National Center for Research to Improve Postsecondary Teaching and Learning (NCRIPTAL) by Stark, Lowther, and others, and another example is the Teaching Goals Inventory developed by Cross and Angelo (1990) at the University of California, Berkeley.

Recommendation 17: Learn more about the systems approach developed by instructional technologists. The field of instructional technology has for decades provided examples of ways to improve teaching. The interested administrator might find Diamond's *Designing and Improving Courses and Curricula in Higher Education* (1989) informative on this topic.

Classroom Observation and Taping

In my experience, few instructors are indifferent about the quality of their instruction. Every college teacher does some mental reviewing about how a class went or what worked or did not work. However, in the press of other responsibilities, most of these reflections are soon forgotten. Classroom observation, especially if combined with videotaping or even audiotaping, provides a permanent record of what went on in the class. The instructor can return to these records later when less busy. These approaches also provide a certain objectivity; to a certain extent, the instructor can "distance" him- or herself and just observe. In addition to permanence and objectivity, classroom observation and taping provide focus. No observation technique or tape can capture everything that goes on in even one class, let alone in an entire course. Of necessity, the teacher must decide what to concentrate on, realizing that many aspects of the course will be ignored.

Recommendation 18: Make taping facilities available to all faculty. It is not enough that taping equipment exists on campus; it must be reasonably accessible for faculty use. Videotaping requires an assistant to work the camera. A common mistake made when videotaping a class is to focus solely on the instructor. If the camera does not frequently pan over the students to show their reactions, at least half of the value of videotaping is lost. Audiotapes will only capture the verbal exchanges, whereas videotapes record nonverbal behaviors as well. The advantages of audiotaping are that the instructor can do it alone and the process is relatively unobtrusive. Notwithstanding the particular drawbacks, either kind of tape provides better data than the instructor's recollection of what took place during the class.

Recommendation 19: Encourage instructors to use classroom observation techniques. Classroom observation techniques can focus on who is talking to whom, on the cognitive level of the questions and answers, or on the emotional quality of the interactions but not on all of these at the same time. First, the instructor must decide what needs improving, why methods may not be working, and what kind of information might help. Often, after gathering one kind of data, you will decide you want to collect or focus on additional kinds of data. A chapter by Evertson and Holley (1981) provides a good introduction to the practical—versus research—uses of classroom observation (see also Cashin, 1988b). It also gives references that describe a wide variety of observation techniques one can choose from. Many of these techniques can be combined with video- or audiotaping. Given today's technology and the increasing availability of VCRs, I prefer to use videotapes. Most instructors find them "data rich," and they can be replayed for a variety of purposes—to reexamine particular parts, to focus on something new, and so on. There is little research on the effectiveness of using videotapes to improve teaching. In his 1976 study, Centra (1979) found that relatively few institutions used videotapes but those that did rated them as especially effective; I have found essentially the same thing (Cashin, 1988b).

Recommendation 20: Encourage instructors to look for positive aspects of their teaching as well as for aspects that need improvement. This may be a problem peculiar to academics, but if we get a 97 on a test, we tend to focus on the 3 points we got wrong. This attitude can make improving teaching a counterproductive experience. Instructors need to be aware of their strengths. Helling (1988) has a classroom observation form that lists only positive aspects of teaching.

Summary

There is a wealth of data available that can be used to improve college teaching. However, only student ratings have received significant attention from researchers. Reviewers of that literature conclude that student ratings are reliable and reasonably valid and unbiased. Therefore, they may be used with considerable confidence as a source of data on which to base decisions about improving teaching. I suggest, however, that student ratings provide information about only a few aspects of teaching and that we in higher education have been limited in our perspective on improving teaching.

A variety of other kinds of data to improve teaching have been discussed in the literature, including course materials, classroom observation, and video- and audiotapes. However, there is little research on their reliability, validity, or usefulness. Until research is conducted, we must rely on our "clinical experience" about the usefulness of these techniques. My experience suggests that these data will also prove very useful in improving college teaching.

References

Arreola, R. A. "Evaluating the Dimensions of Teaching." *Instructional Evaluation*, 1986, *8*, 4–12.

Braskamp, L. A., Brandenburg, D. C., and Ory, J. C. *Evaluating Teaching Effectiveness: A Practical Guide.* Newbury Park, Calif.: Sage, 1984.

Cashin, W. E. *Student Ratings of Teaching: A Summary of the Research.* IDEA paper no. 20. Manhattan: Center for Faculty Evaluation and Development, Kansas State University, 1988a. (ERIC no. ED 302 567)

Cashin, W. E. "Using Evaluation Data to Improve College Classroom Teaching." In I. S. Cohen (ed.), *The G. Stanley Hall Lecture Series.* Vol. 8. Washington, D.C.: American Psychological Association, 1988b.

Cashin, W. E. *Defining and Evaluating College Teaching.*

IDEA Paper no. 21. Manhattan: Kansas State University, Center for Faculty Evaluation and Development, 1989.

Centra, J. A. *Determining Faculty Effectiveness: Assessing Teaching, Research, and Service for Personnel Decisions and Improvement.* San Francisco: Jossey-Bass, 1979.

Cross, K. P., and Angelo, T. *Teaching Goals Inventory.* Berkeley: School of Education, University of California, 1990.

Diamond, R. M. *Designing and Improving Courses and Curricula in Higher Education.* San Francisco: Jossey-Bass, 1989.

Evertson, C. M., and Holley, F. M. "Classroom Observation." In J. Millman (ed.), *Handbook of Teacher Evaluation.* Newbury Park, Calif.: Sage, 1981.

Helling, B. B. "Looking for Good Teaching: A Guide to Peer Observation." *Journal of Staff, Program, and Organizational Development,* 1988, *6,* 147–158.

Marsh, H. W. "Students' Evaluations of University Teaching: Dimensionality, Reliability, Validity, Potential Biases, and Utility." *Journal of Educational Psychology,* 1984, *76,* 707–754.

Miller, R. I. *Evaluating Faculty for Promotion and Tenure.* San Francisco: Jossey-Bass, 1987.

Seldin, P. *Successful Faculty Evaluation Programs: A Practical Guide to Improve Faculty Performance and Promotion/Tenure Decisions.* Crugers, N.Y.: Coventry Press, 1980.

Seldin, P. *Changing Practices in Faculty Evaluation: A Critical Assessment and Recommendations for Improvement.* San Francisco: Jossey-Bass, 1984.

CHAPTER 6

Using Evaluative Information to Improve Instruction

Robert J. Menges

Complaints about evaluation pervade education. Faculty complain about salary decisions: "There isn't enough information to judge how well I teach!" Junior faculty complain about tenure decisions: "They keep raising the standards!" Everybody complains about filling out forms and filing reports: "What do they do with all this information?" It sometimes seems that there is more interest in evaluating teachers than in improving teaching effectiveness.

The problem is intensified because administrators fill dual roles. On the one hand, administrators are allies of the faculty, attempting to diagnose and solve teaching problems in a supportive way. On the other hand, administrators make significant organizational decisions. They can remove incompetent teachers, and they control rewards for effective teaching. Understandably, this makes faculty somewhat defensive; no one takes big risks when the boss is around. Faculty worry that evaluative information intended for self-improvement may be used for personnel review. Consequently, improvements may not be specific enough to yield evaluative information.

If evaluations are to improve teaching, faculty must know who is in charge of evaluative information, and the evaluation must focus on a manageable part of the instructional process. In this chapter, I argue that the teacher should be in charge of information when the goal is improvement, and I present a model of the instructional process that helps focus improvement efforts.

The Many Senses of Evaluation

Our colleges and universities are evaluation prone. These evaluations range from cynical attempts at manipulating the institution's image to well-meaning efforts at enhancing the experiences of teachers and learners. The purposes of evaluations also vary and sometimes conflict.

Evaluations that emphasize information about teaching may serve at least four purposes. As shown in Table 1, teaching-based evaluation information may serve institutional accreditation, students, personnel review, and instructional improvement. Table 1 specifies these purposes in relation to the users of the information and lists the evidence showing that the evaluation has had a positive effect.

In accreditation reviews, for example, information about teaching addresses teaching load, class size, student satisfaction, and so on. This information is communicated to the reviewing agency and, if adequate, leads to prompt accreditation approval.

In personnel review, evaluations differ in important ways from those intended to improve instruction. As seen in Table 1, the latter generate information for use by the teacher, whereas the former generate information for use by administrators. Indicators of success also differ. Improved student learning is the best evidence of improved instruction. The success of personnel review, however, is shown primarily by greater faculty productivity, of which student learning is only one part.

Confusion and conflict occur when evaluators fail to make their assumptions explicit. In the hundreds of books and articles about faculty evaluation, terms are often used imprecisely: "The language of faculty evaluation is riddled

Table 1. Evaluative Information About Teaching.

Purpose	Users	Effect
Accrediting institutions	Accreditation agencies	Prompt and positive accreditation decisions
Informing students	Students	Better match of students with program/course/instructor
Reviewing personnel	Administrators	Greater faculty productivity
Improving instruction	Faculty	More and better student learning

with vagueness and ambiguity" (Riegle and Rhodes, 1986, p. 123). Confusion inevitably results when those who write about evaluation and those who make evaluative decisions fail to specify the metaphors that underlie their positions. Riegle and Rhodes distinguish five such metaphors. The metaphor of assessing, for example, calls to mind examination of a piece of land that has not yet been fully developed. A decision about the value of the land must take into account its potential features as well as its actual features, and these must be viewed in light of its intended use. In academia, the assessment metaphor is applicable to tenure reviews but is not appropriate for reviewing teachers for salary, promotion, and tenure decisions or for reviewing teaching for self-improvement.

When teaching improvement is the purpose of evaluation, the most appropriate metaphor, according to Riegle and Rhodes, is critiquing. The critic observes the teacher at work and offers a critical review. This information is used by the teacher to make decisions about improving future performance.

The least appropriate metaphor for evaluations aimed at improving teaching is the metaphor of judging. Under the judging metaphor, the teacher becomes "a defendant who must present his or her case as persuasively as possible" (Riegle and Rhodes, 1986, p. 123). The judge—presumably an administrator—reviews evidence and testimony and renders a verdict. This adversarial situation is sure to stimulate faculty defensiveness, since teachers may feel they are being treated as objects of evaluation.

For improvement purposes, it is the teacher who should control evaluative information and make evaluative decisions. Such decisions are not ends in themselves; they are means toward improvement.

My advice to administrators is that acting as a judge is likely to be counterproductive when instructional improvement is the intended purpose. A sympathetic administrator may certainly facilitate evaluation and improvement, but control should reside with the teacher.

The Many Settings for Teaching and Learning

Although most teaching occurs in the classroom, most learning does not. A great deal of learning occurs out of the presence of the teacher. Learning may occur in libraries, laboratories, studios, study rooms, and living areas. Indeed, learning may occur in any setting where learners encounter the subject matter for study.

The job of the teacher is to be cognizant of all those settings, using them to shape an environment conducive to learning. The essence of teaching is the creation of situations in which appropriate learning occurs; shaping those situations is what successful teachers have learned to do effectively (Menges, 1981).

Evaluation is made no easier when we characterize teaching in this complex, multivariate way. Evaluation of teaching requires that we isolate pertinent variables and also that we consider how those variables fit together. As Menges and Mathis (1988, p. 10) note:

Effectiveness in teaching depends not on a single characteristic but on the appropriate fit among many variables. These variables include the purposes of the teaching-learning encounter, characteristics and preferences of teachers and learners, circumstances of the teaching-learning activities and of the larger environment in which those activities occur, and methods used for determining success of the teaching and of the learning. Effective teachers monitor and manage all of these variables, ensure their consistency and fashion them into a pleasing whole.

To improve instruction, it is not enough to have information of a general kind, such as summary ratings of teaching. Information must be specific and diagnostic; that is, it should identify what ought to be changed and imply what kinds of changes would be effective.

The Four Ps Model of Instruction

To guide evaluation, we need a model that distinguishes among major components of the instructional process and suggests what information is appropriate for diagnosing and strengthening each component. Further, the model must assemble the components into a whole that is coherently organized around the teacher, who acts as the center of the instructional process.

The four Ps model depicts the instructional process and provides a guide for instructional planning and evaluation. It is also useful in workshops for graduate students and colleagues. The model postulates four components of instruction: preconditions, plans, procedures, and products.

Preconditions. Preconditions are the circumstances that prevail before any teaching and learning occur. Information about preconditions includes information about subject matter, physical facilities, learners, and the teacher.

Regarding subject matter, it is helpful to know the institutional history of the course and the expectations currently held about it. How do institutional documents, such as catalogues and curriculum plans, describe the course? Where is the course placed within the curriculum? What do administrators and faculty expect of the course? This information must be obtained from the institutional memory either through archival records or from authoritative informants.

As concerns physical facilities, instruction benefits from information about classroom location, layout, and capacity; library resources and regulations; equipment for laboratory experiments and computer work; and audiovisual services. Many a course has started badly because books were not available for students to purchase or because too few reserve copies of readings were accessible at the library, or—most embarrassing of all—because the teacher found the classroom door locked or, once inside, searched in vain for a piece of chalk. It is far better to identify discrepancies between needed and available facilities in advance, when time remains either to modify facilities or to alter plans.

Information about learners is critical but may be difficult to obtain. Some is fairly obvious, such as the number of students enrolled, their previous work in related courses, and their aptitude. Other information concerns more subtle matters, such as students' expectations of the course, their preferred style of learning, and their degree of intellectual development. Relevant information may be available from the registrar's office or from an institutional testing program, but rarely is this information communicated to faculty sufficiently far in advance. The makeup of a class may not be known until its first meeting; if pretests devised by the instructor are not administered until that time, they can be used only to make last-minute minor adjustments.

Characteristics of the teacher, like the other preconditions, predate instruction. Planning can be facilitated when instructors reflect on their beliefs about teaching, including beliefs about the proper role and behavior of teachers and students; when instructors assess their preferences and skills regarding teaching methods; and when instructors learn more about the norms related to teaching that prevail in the organization (for example, the proportion of time an untenured teacher is expected to allocate to teaching compared with scholarship or service). To the disadvantage of our students, few faculty learn these things until they have been teaching for some time. It is far preferable that instruction be planned in light of this information.

Plans. With information about preconditions available, the teacher can proceed to codify plans. Following the systems approach to instructional design, the teacher states general goals for the course and constructs a comprehensive list of intended learning outcomes. To focus on plans is to acknowledge that one cannot devise a route for the instructional journey until the destination has been specified.

Plans take the form of statements (1) about what learners will know or be able to do at the conclusion of instruction (performance objectives) and (2) about activities that enable learners to attain the appropriate level of knowledge and skills (enabling objectives). Even those who believe that some important learning outcomes cannot be specified in advance are likely to agree that attempting to identify them is a worthwhile exercise, as long as subsequent modifications and additions are permitted.

Goals and objectives can form an important part of the course syllabus. Such information is much more useful than the brief schedule of topics and assignments comprising the syllabus for many courses. Students need to know what they are expected to do and the deadlines for doing it, but they can assess the adequacy of their learning only if they are informed about expected performance.

In this sense, plans are learner focused rather than teacher focused. Instead of selecting learning activities on the basis of the question "What shall I do in class today?" the teacher selects activities that are appropriate for the stated learning outcomes, asking "How should students be different at the conclusion of this course (or after today's class or after turning in this assignment)?"

The teacher is the primary source of information about instructional plans.

Procedures. Procedures refer to events that occur when learners interact with subject matter. Many of these events happen in the presence and under the direct instruction of the teacher, such as classroom lectures, discussion, and examinations. For other events, such as completing assigned readings, solving homework problems, writing essays, designing research projects, and other assignments, the teacher is not present.

Instructional procedures include three phases: exposure, practice, and feedback. In the first phase, the learner is exposed to the subject matter through teacher presentations, discussions with peers, reading, and so on. In the second phase, the learner works with the subject matter, processing, manipulating, and transforming it. Depending on the instructor's objectives, practice may require recall of information, application of concepts and principles, analysis and synthesis of major ideas, evaluation of arguments and theories, or generation of novel examples and applications. In the third phase, learners receive feedback about the adequacy of their practice. From this feedback, both teacher and learner can determine when it is appropriate to move on to new subject matter.

To be comprehensive, information about instructional procedures should touch on all three phases: exposure, practice, and feedback. This requires information beyond what is immediately known to the teacher. In the classroom, teachers are too busy to be aware of all salient details. When students are outside of the classroom, teachers have no access to their opinions and behaviors. Nevertheless, students are quite willing to provide information through questionnaires and interviews. They may even be persuaded to keep journals of their study practices. Students and colleagues are easily trained to be reliable observers and recorders of classroom events. Audio and video recordings permit access to classroom occurrences at a later time, when they can be examined at leisure.

Products. The residues that remain when a teaching-learning experience has ended constitute the products of instruction. These residues include knowledge, skills, and attitudes. Information most directly related to products is best acquired from learners themselves. Examinations and other graded material routinely document knowledge acquisition. Information about complex learning outcomes is less readily available, but may refer to critical thinking, independent learning, problem identification, problem solving, and assimilation of course materials into personal standards and values. Even when learning outcome information is available for a particular course, we may be unable to determine what part of the outcome should be attributed to that particular teacher and course.

Student attitudes about the teacher and course are routinely documented in end-of-course questionnaires given to students. This information can often be compared with norms of the department or institution.

These four components of the instructional process are displayed in Figure 1. Dotted arrows show patterns for a conventional linear approach to instructional design. In this approach, plans are developed in light of preconditions. Then procedures are generated from plans. Finally, information about products is fed into the next planning cycle. Yet this conventional model is misleading because it fails to reveal the dominant, active role of the teacher. In reality, the college teacher is often owner of the course and sovereign in the classroom.

To improve the accuracy of this model, the teacher should be placed in the center. The teacher generates plans in light of preconditions and self-analysis, shapes procedures that are congruent with those plans, devises ways to document products, and determines whether the knowledge, skills, and attitudes of students are consistent with course plans. Finally, it is the teacher who renders judgments about the relative success of the instructional experience.

Solving Instructional Problems Using Evaluative Information

Each component of the four Ps model can aid in distinctive ways in solving instructional problems. The examples in this chapter are composites drawn from my own experience. More extensive cases can be found in the practical literature on teaching improvement. This literature is surveyed in *Key Resources on Teaching, Learning, Curriculum,*

Figure 1. The Four Ps Model of Instruction.

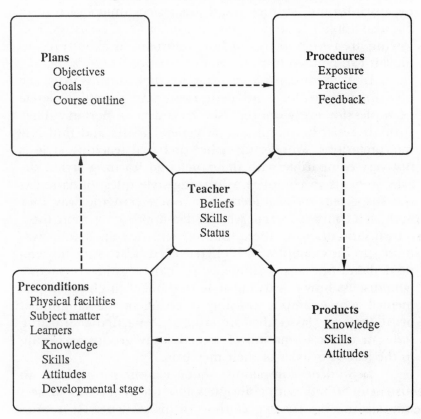

and *Faculty Development* (Menges and Mathis, 1988) and *Key Resources on Community College* (Cohen, Palmer, and Zwemer, 1986). These volumes also include lists of journals concerned with teaching in various disciplines and professional fields. Among other useful sources are publications of the Professional and Organizational Development Network in Higher Education and the National Association for Staff, Program, and Organizational Development.

Improving Instruction Using Information About Preconditions. Information gathered prior to the beginning of instruction sometimes anticipates important instructional problems. This point is most obvious for information about the institution's facilities and the expected content of courses but also applies to student and instructor characteristics. Following are two examples of how information about preconditions can be used to improve instruction.

1. A discouraged teacher reports that students insist she give them word-for-word definitions and several concrete examples for every concept she considers important. They strongly resist her emphasis on general issues and multiple interpretations. Wondering if her preferred teaching style is not very compatible with their preferred learning styles, she asks students to complete a learning-style questionnaire. As she suspected, most students are concrete in the way they approach course material, whereas her approach is more theoretical. She discusses these findings with the class and gives more specific examples and concrete exercises to students who need them. She also volunteers to chair a group of faculty who discuss how a learning-style assessment might be implemented across campus, possibly resulting in the assignment of students to classes that are tailored to particular learning styles or to the formation of special study groups according to the learning styles of their members.

2. Student complaints about examinations lead an instructor to talk with colleagues about how the way he sees himself matches the expectations of his students. At a series of lunchtime meetings, they discuss a typology of teaching, which delineates several teacher orientations: teacher as expert, facilitator, formal authority, professional gatekeeper, and so on. He realizes that he teaches his introductory course as a gatekeeper. That is, he treats virtually all students as potential majors in the department and potential professionals in his field, although few actually take more than one or two courses in that discipline. After further discussion about the intended curricular function of the course, he decides to revise his course objectives and make substantial changes in readings, assignments, and examinations.

These examples show how attention to preconditions can improve instruction. More information about student learning styles can lead to more appropriate learning procedures. Discussion and reflection concerning teacher and student roles can lead to learning objectives that better serve the expectations of faculty and the needs of individual students.

Improving Instruction Using Information About Plans. As a component of the instructional model, plans include curricular issues about subject matter to be covered and pedagogical issues about how the expected outcomes of courses can be conveyed to students and colleagues.

1. A department chair hears many students comment that the same material is covered in several of the department's courses. Each instructor apparently assumes the topic is new to students, and students say they receive repeated introductions to the same topics that never move beyond the elementary level. Teachers of these courses decide to compare syllabi and determine the extent of overlap. They consider the merits of requiring students to take courses in a uniform sequence or of requiring students who do not follow that sequence to complete special assignments. As a result of the discussions, teachers become much more specific about what knowledge and skills are expected of learners each time they encounter these topics.

2. A teacher nearing tenure review is told of departmental concerns that his teaching methods are too loose—that is, that students seem to be choosing almost any topic as a basis for their readings and term papers. Consequently, few students cover the same basic material. The teacher realizes that he has not been sufficiently explicit about the educational goals he values most highly—namely, independent learning and critical thinking. In his syllabus, he clarifies those expectations and tells students that to reach these goals they must choose their own topics and pursue those topics as they wish. He attempts to deal with his colleagues' concern about content coverage by requiring students to read and comment on one another's work.

3. In an introductory survey course, students constantly ask the instructor how much of the readings they are respon-

sible for. In attempting to eliminate these questions, she revises her objectives so that they specify the concepts that students must define and apply. She also devises homework assignments that require students to analyze and evaluate major ideas and includes these materials in the syllabus as self-tests. This greatly reduces student questions. In fact, the approach works so well that next year she plans to substitute for the major course examinations a series of six mastery tests based on homework assignments.

In each of these examples, instruction was improved by attention to plans: analyzing content covered in core courses, making general goals more specific, preparing specific learning objectives, and deriving learning exercises from them.

Improving Instruction Using Information About Procedures. In the four Ps model, procedures refer to events that occur when students are dealing directly with the subject matter they are expected to master. The following examples focus on each of the three phases of instructional procedures: exposure, practice, and feedback.

1. A teacher suspects that students are not learning lecture content that is not also covered in course readings, and his analysis of selected examination questions confirms that impression. After reviewing videotapes of class sessions, he identifies two reasons students may fail to master this information even though they have been exposed to it.

First, he realizes how difficult it is for students to read the messy chalkboard. To solve this problem, he tries to write larger, but this leads students to protest his frequent erasures. He then experiments with transparencies but feels that they constrain his "spontaneous" teaching style. Finally, he returns to the chalkboard but gives each student an outline of his notes, including definitions of key terms and a copy of each chart and figure he constructs on the board.

The tapes also reveal that he rarely points out to students which information from the lectures is not in their readings. In notes subsequently prepared for students, an asterisk denotes items covered only in lectures. A check of subsequent examinations shows that students now perform as well on lecture-only information as on other questions.

2. From occasional conversations outside of class, a teacher realizes that students have only a superficial understanding of some material she wants them to apply to new situations. She invites a colleague to a couple of class sessions to analyze the class interaction patterns and to take notes on the content of discussions. To her surprise, he reports that eight of the forty students in the class account for nearly 80 percent of all student talk and that teacher talk time is at least twice that of student talk time, even during discussion portions of the class. Further, discussion deals primarily with matters of fact rather than matters of application.

To solve this problem, she devises exercises that require students to practice applying course information to new problems. Her class now begins with a presentation of no more than ten minutes. A half hour is then devoted to small groups that work on the application problem. Discussions by the whole class during the remaining time are quite animated, involve a larger proportion of students, and devote more time to applications than to memorized information. On examinations, students do better with those questions that call for application of course material.

3. An instructor is concerned that students show little improvement in their graded work during the term. Interviews with small groups of students reveal that, although they work harder for each subsequent assignment, they do not know how to work better. The teacher believes that they need more diagnostic and frequent feedback, but he lacks time to grade and comment on additional student work. In the future, he plans to make a battery of practice problems and essay assignments available on the computer, using programs that comment on the grammar, spelling, and style of student writing as well as on the accuracy of solutions. Until the computer system is up and running, he requires students to work on these problems in pairs. Although he checks only a few papers on a random basis, each student knows that at

least two assignments will count toward the course grade. This activity ensures that students gain practice working with course material, and the feedback students give each other enhances their mastery even further. In fact, students' work now shows considerable improvement as the course proceeds.

These examples show that instructional problems can be solved by attention to procedures: using videotape to help an instructor determine that information to which students are exposed is actually learned, preparing exercises through which students practice applying course information to new problems, using feedback from peers to help students understand how well they have mastered course content.

Improving Instruction Using Information About Products. In the four Ps model, products refer to the knowledge, skills, and attitudes that remain after instruction is concluded. The above examples show that product information, such as end-of-course student questionnaires or examination scores, is often useful for improving plans or procedures. In the examples below, it is product information itself that must be improved.

1. A department chair reminds a third-year teacher that her course evaluations have been consistently below the evaluations of others in the department. Although she is concerned about poor evaluations, she feels frustrated because information from the questionnaires is quite general; it does not imply what changes should be made or how to determine whether changes are successful. A friend who consults about teaching in another department gives her a catalogue of questionnaire items that refer to quite specific behaviors, and she selects several to add to the standard evaluation form. She also prepares open-ended questions on issues of particular concern, including: "I do my best work in this course when the teacher . . ." "I feel most involved in the class when I . . ." Finally, a diagnostic form for midterm feedback is drafted, with items keyed to the particular changes she has made for that term.

Faculty in other departments express interest in what

she is doing, and modifications are planned for the college's course and teacher evaluation program. In the future, each teacher will be able to add items selected from the catalogue to the collegewide form, and the additions can vary from term to term and from course to course. Some items in the catalogue are accompanied by suggestions about particular teaching techniques that have been associated with especially high ratings. Consultation is available to help faculty interpret evaluation results and to design questionnaires that can be used at midterm or that focus on distinctive aspects of the course. Results of the supplementary items are released solely to the faculty member.

2. The employment success of several recent graduates who created an ad hoc major prompts several departments to begin planning a formal major in that field, but faculty realize that little information about alumni is available to departments for program development. They prepare a survey for groups of alumni selected at five-year intervals that will reveal more about graduates' employment history. In addition, they plan to convene several focus groups to gather reactions of recent graduates to the proposed new major.

These examples show how information about the products of instruction can help to improve instruction: adapting a course evaluation system so that it serves faculty self-improvement as well as institutional personnel review and making better use of information about alumni employment for program development.

The Administrator's Role

In most of the examples in this chapter, the main actors are teachers; administrators play a supporting role. Following are some ways administrators might demonstrate their support of evaluative information for improving teaching:

• Establish lunchtime conversations in which participants present their biggest instructional failures for discussion. At the first meeting, an administrator is the presenter.

- Create a collection of books, articles, and videotapes about effective teaching and place these items in the faculty lounge.
- Publicize campus agencies that support teaching, provide modest resources to faculty who wish to use these agencies, and keep the interactions confidential.
- Host annual visits by an external consultant who will work in confidence with individual teachers about teaching problems and help them design their own evaluations.
- See that each new member of the faculty has a mentor during the first year of adjustment to new colleagues, students, and courses.
- Expect every teacher to report formally each year on improvements to at least one course, including information about what was changed and the differences those changes have made for students.

In summary, administrators should establish a climate where instructional evaluation is expected, and they should cultivate norms that encourage faculty to invest time and energy in instructional improvement. Teachers should choose what information is pertinent to instructional evaluation, devise improvements, and monitor their implementation. Administrators should see that a variety of information about instruction can be easily gathered, but teachers should manage that information. Administrators should engage consultants who assist teachers as they interpret evaluative data and devise and monitor improvements, but the consultant's services should be only at the request of teachers. Administrators should ensure that rewards for effective teaching are frequent and generous, but evidence of improved instruction should come from teachers.

Administrators can cultivate communication and collaboration about teaching and its improvement without surrendering their responsibility for making evaluative decisions. Ultimately, however, administrators defer to the teacher on many matters of pedagogy, just as teachers defer to administrators as the final authority on many matters of management.

References

Cohen, A. M., Palmer, J. C., and Zwemer, K. D. *Key Resources on Community Colleges.* San Francisco: Jossey-Bass, 1986.

Menges, R. J. "Instructional Methods." In A. W. Chickering and Associates (eds.), *The Modern American College.* San Francisco: Jossey-Bass, 1981.

Menges, R. J., and Mathis, B. C. *Key Resources on Teaching, Learning, Curriculum, and Faculty Development.* San Francisco: Jossey-Bass, 1988.

Riegle, R. P., and Rhodes, D. M. "Avoiding Mixed Metaphors of Faculty Evaluation." *College Teaching,* 1986, *34,* 123–128.

CHAPTER 7

Classroom Research: Helping Professors Learn More About Teaching and Learning

K. Patricia Cross

The educational reform movement, initiated in 1983 by the National Commission on Excellence in Education publication of *A Nation at Risk,* changed the role of college administrators from managers to educational leaders. While this introductory statement may be somewhat overdrawn, it is nonetheless true that the work of college administrators is influenced in large measure by the times in which they work.

In the 1960s, college administrators were dealing with enormous growth in college enrollments. Administrators directed their energies to the building of buildings, the recruitment of large numbers of faculty members, and, in general, the expansion of resources, programs, and facilities. The late 1970s found higher education still dealing with numbers, but this time it was with decline or the threat of decline. Harder than the satisfying work of building was the frustrating task of retrenchment, the deferred maintenance of buildings, the contraction of faculty and programs. The administrative requirements for the 1960s and 1970s were largely managerial, calling for skills in the acquisition and/or conservation of resources to handle the expansion or contraction of higher education.

Many readers are familiar with the classic distinction between efficiency and effectiveness. Efficiency consists of doing things right, whereas effectiveness consists of doing the right things. Ideally, administrators would combine efficiency with effectiveness by doing the right things right. But by and large, we in education have been concentrating more on managing colleges efficiently than on making them effective; that is, we have been paying more attention to doing things right than to doing the right things. Although some might question how efficiently colleges have been managed, trustees, legislators, and the public they represent are more concerned today about the effectiveness of higher education.

One sign of the rising concern about the effectiveness of education is the emphasis on assessment. By 1987, two-thirds of the states had introduced assessment initiatives (Boyer and others, 1987), and 79 percent of the campus administrators polled by the American Council on Education said that they expected some form of assessment to be introduced on their campus within the next few years (El-Khawas, 1987). The emphasis on educational effectiveness, accompanied by the growth of the assessment movement, has swept the nation with remarkable speed, considering the number of people affected and the decision-making mechanisms involved. Although the general purpose of assessment is the eventual improvement in the quality of education, there are two quite distinctive goals in the assessment movement. Both goals have implications for educational leadership.

One goal might be called assessment for accountability; the other, assessment for improvement. Missouri governor John Ashcroft, who chaired the Governor's Task Force on College Quality, speaks for accountability, noting, "The public has the right to know what it is getting for its expenditure of tax resources; the public has a right to know and understand the quality of undergraduate education that young people receive from publicly funded colleges and universities" (National Governors' Association, 1986, p. 154).

The assessment-for-improvement perspective is expressed by William Turnbull (1985, p. 25), late president of Educational Testing Service, who commented, "The overriding purpose of gathering [assessment] data is to provide a basis for improving instruction, rather than keeping score or allocating blame."

Although the ultimate goal of both types of assessment is the improvement of education, feedback is handled quite differently in the two models. In the accountability model, feedback is usually public, normative, comparative, and competitive. As Governor Ashcraft noted, the public has a right to know, and this implies that they have a right to compare programs competing for funds. Assessment for accountability is also summative in the sense that it provides a "stop-motion" summary of the situation at any given point in time. Assessment measures may be taken at the end of the freshman year, at the end of two or four years of college, or even from alumni five or ten years after graduation. The purpose of the information is to document the effectiveness of education and, ultimately, to correct deficiencies.

In contrast, the role of feedback in the assessment-for-improvement model is to provide a continuous flow of information that is useful in shaping the quality of teaching of learning while it is in process. This is generally referred to as formative evaluation, and feedback is most effective if it is not made public and if it emphasizes competencies instead of comparisons.

A second distinction can be made between direct and indirect models of assessment. Those who, by virtue of their positions, are interested in accountability usually have indirect responsibilities for teaching and learning. That is, they are not on the campus or in the classroom and must try in whatever ways they can to influence the behavior of those who are in a position to affect teaching and learning directly. It follows that the further removed one is from the scene of the action in teaching and learning, the more one is dependent on manipulating reward and punishment to bring about desired ends. States manipulate rewards for institutions; institutions manipulate rewards for departments; departments manipulate rewards for teachers. Thus, the motivation for improvement in indirect models of assessment is usually extrinsic—promotion, tenure, and a teacher-of-the-year award for good teachers and lack of reward (rather than punishment) for poor teachers.

College administrators, by and large, have found themselves dealing largely with assessment for accountability by indirect means. That is, they are being held accountable for something they cannot control directly. What, then, can administrators do to improve the quality of education?

It is my contention that if we are serious about educational reform, teachers must assume more personal responsibility for what is taught and learned in their own classrooms. That means that the assessment movement must be made the direct responsibility of teachers. One way to do this is to involve teachers in classroom research. By classroom research, I mean systematic and insightful observation about how students learn.

The purpose of classroom research is to provide feedback, insights, and understandings to classroom teachers about how students learn the particular subject matter. If we can help teachers assess the learning of their own students, we will go a long way toward establishing accountability in education. The ultimate goal of classroom research is to make teaching more productive—that is, to reduce the gap between what is taught and what is learned (Cross, 1988). Classroom research was founded on the premise that if they can monitor what students are learning, teachers can determine the effectiveness of their teaching and can modify it accordingly.

An example of a very simple form of classroom assessment will make the concept concrete. "Minute papers" is an assessment technique developed by a physics professor at the University of California, Berkeley (Wilson, 1986). A few minutes before the end of the class period, the instructor asks students to write the answers to two questions: (1) What was the most important thing you learned today? and (2) What questions remain uppermost in your mind as we conclude this session? (Other examples of simple classroom assessment techniques can be found in Cross and Angelo, 1988.)

Teachers using this simple device can assess the response of students to a particular class session. There are also two important pedagogical devices embedded in this technique. Students are asked to summarize what has been learned, and they are also "put on notice" that they are expected to be actively involved in learning and in raising their own questions about their mastery of the subject matter. Classroom assessment usually asks these rather simple questions: How well can students paraphrase the major points emphasized in the class session? How much of the terminology of this discipline do they remember from one class session to the next? and How well do they make comparisons and analyze arguments? The assessment techniques used in answering these questions teach as well as test. If a teacher wants to know how well students can analyze an argument, for example, the assessment technique must engage students in the analysis of an argument.

A few examples of classroom research projects that have been carried out by teachers with whom we have worked will help to illustrate the role of assessment in providing feedback to the classroom teacher:

A precalculus teacher in a community college had long been troubled by the extreme diversity of students' backgrounds in math, so prior to teaching each new unit, he developed a brief questionnaire to determine students' familiarity with the procedures and terminology of the new material. With this "background probe" and his analysis of the data collected, he could anticipate where students would run into difficulties and could modify his teaching accordingly. He reported that an unanticipated benefit of his classroom research was students' appreciation of his concern and interest in their background.

In another example, an English teacher was never quite sure what students were really learning from small-group sessions in which the task was to critique one anothers' papers. She used a modification of minute papers, asking students to take a few minutes at the end of the class period to write the answers to these two questions: (1) What have you learned today about your own writing? and (2) What did you contribute to the learning of others in the group? A side benefit of her study was that students, knowing that they were going to be asked about their learning, paid increased attention to the tasks of the small groups and, not so incidentally, paid much more attention than they had previously to thinking about how they could be helpful and constructive in their critiques of their classmates' writing.

A final example will make clear the pedagogy behind the assessment tasks that teachers are using in early stages of classroom research. The primary purpose of a course in third-semester calculus was to prepare students for advanced courses in engineering and physics. The question the teacher of this course chose to investigate was whether students were, in fact, able to apply their learning in math to science concepts. He collected examples of simple applications from colleagues in the science department and determined how well students could handle these; he then experimented to see how he could help students learn more effectively. A side benefit of his project was the conversation and collaboration of teachers across departments.

Experience shows that many teachers proceed rather quickly from these fairly simple investigations in assessment to more complex research designs that are of interest in their particular discipline.

The purpose and the methods of classroom research are quite different from more traditional educational research. The purpose is not to discover general laws of learning (which is the task of more traditional educational research) nor to enhance the research reputations or publications records of classroom teachers. Rather, the purpose is to help teachers gain insight into how students respond to their teaching methods and how students learn the particular subject matter. Because of this specific focus, classroom research does not require sophisticated statistics or knowledge of sampling theory, since classroom researchers are not trying to select a sample and generalize to the population at large. Classroom research poses one specific question: What are *my* students learning in *my* classroom as a result of *my* instruction? Classroom research is based in two traditions of improving teaching—educational research and faculty development—but it differs in important respects from both of these approaches.

After more than eighty years and thousands of research studies, it is hard to say what we know from research that has changed the way teachers teach. It is not just that research is not written for practitioners or that practitioners do not read the research but rather that practitioners consider research findings irrelevant. One noted educational researcher put it this way: "Thus, those who are best informed about educational research seldom use the fruits of their labors. . . . If educational researchers do not use research findings to guide their own professional decisions, why should we expect those less well informed to use research findings to guide theirs?" (Eisner, 1984, p. 256).

Critics of educational research are quick to point to some major problems, and there is not much doubt that research in the social sciences, in general, and education, in particular, is undergoing massive, albeit slow, change. Older generations of educational researchers were impressed with the great scientific advances made in the physical sciences, and they not only named their endeavor the social sciences, in emulation of the so-called hard sciences, but they also tried to apply the methods of the sciences—tightly controlled experiments and a search for universal laws or generalizations applicable across a variety of situations.

When I was in graduate school, psychology was dominated by B. F. Skinner and the behaviorists. Psychology was a science, we insisted, and we could not study what we could not observe. We believed in stimulus-response, or S-R, theories of learning. There was a measurable stimulus and an observable response that all animals—monkeys, pigeons, and people—made with some regularity. Given sufficient persistence, we thought, we could discover some universal laws of behavior. This school of psychology casts learning into a black box, so called because we did not know (and certainly we thought it unscientific to study) what went on in the mind of the learner.

Now a new generation of cognitive psychologists has emerged, and they care deeply about what goes on in the mind of the learner. Moreover, they really do not mind asking people what is going on in what was formerly the black box of the mind. One of the more exciting branches of research on learning today focuses on metacognition, which is a study of how learners monitor and direct their own learning.

Classroom research belongs to this branch of the educational research family in that it recognizes the importance of getting feedback from learners on what is going on in their minds. How do they perceive the learning situation? What, in fact, are they learning and how well? How aware are they of themselves as learners? Do they monitor their own thinking processes? Are they able to tell us or show us what kinds of teaching have an impact on their learning?

However, there is an important difference between the goals of cognitive psychology and classroom research. Educational researchers who study metacognition are still searching for universals. For example, they would like to show that students who monitor their learning are significantly better learners than those who do not. These researchers use a basically scientistic model, searching for prediction and control. A general law of learning might be stated in this way: *If* we can teach students to monitor their learning, *then* we can produce more effective learning.

Although classroom researchers are certainly interested in any such finding—that is, interested in benefiting from the experience and knowledge of educational research—the curiosity of classroom researchers is directed more toward insight and understanding than toward prediction and control. Classroom researchers, for example, are not looking for a law of human behavior that will provide an if/then formula that will tell them that *if* they teach in a certain way, *then* a certain kind of learning will occur—or even that such learning will occur predictably in 62 percent of the cases. Classroom researchers are primarily interested in gaining the insights and understandings that will strengthen their base of professional knowledge about teaching. They want to know what works, of course, but they are even more interested in knowing why it works. They want to understand learning as a process, and they consider insights as important as findings.

Every once in a while, someone becomes interested in teacher-proof education—that is, in devising some presumably research-based rule or formula that if applied as researchers direct will result consistently in improved learning. Although we sometimes speak erroneously of teacher training as though teachers, like pigeons, can be trained to respond in predictable ways, we should be talking about teacher education or, better yet, the professionalization of teaching.

The major characteristic of a profession is that it depends on the wise and effective use of judgment and knowledge. No one can tell a teacher what to do next, since the classroom environment varies from minute to minute. What the teacher does next depends on his or her skill, experience, professional knowledge, and insight. There are few rules that can be applied and few situations in laboratory or experimental conditions can be duplicated in the classroom. Thus classroom researchers aim at professionalizing teaching through increasing insight and understanding rather than through scientifically controlled experiments that search for universals.

Freeing classroom research from the search for universals has a number of advantages for the professional teacher. First, one of the firm rules of science is that findings must be replicable. Any other scientist anywhere in the world, following the same procedures as the initial investigator, must be able to come up with the same results.

Replication in education is hard to achieve. Teachers and students are not replicable; no two teachers have the same classrooms or the same students. Thus, we in educational research tend to depend on probability and repetition to verify findings. If x number of physics teachers teach y to 100 students, and 67 percent of them respond in a consistent way, then we have to be content with the conclusion that the finding is valid most of the time.

Some probability conclusions are quite elegant; others are enormously complex and require enormous amounts of data and analysis to support their case. Following is an example of one of the more elegant and useful, but frequently ignored findings, from educational research that is equally applicable to classroom research.

We have known for at least fifty years that the curve is steep for how much information presented in a lecture form is forgotten by students. In 1923 Harold Jones demonstrated that the average student could recall about 62 percent of the lecture material immediately following the lecture, about 45 percent after three or four days, and only 24 percent after eight weeks. If students took an examination immediately following the lecture, however, they retained almost twice as much material after eight weeks, both for thought questions and for fact questions. (This classic experiment was called to my attention by Robert Menges, 1988.)

That finding from educational research could be made into a general law of learning that would state that people remember what they do longer than what they are told, or that students actively involved in coming up with their own answers remember the material longer than when answers are given to them, or that material recalled under conditions that are moderately anxiety producing is remembered longer than when conditions are less threatening. Whatever the underlying rationale (and that could be systematically investigated), the probability is fairly high that if a teacher gave a final examination with half of the questions taken from the midterm and half new questions of equal difficulty, students would get higher scores on the repeat questions.

That is what I call an elegant experiment in educational research, as applicable to classroom researchers as to expensive, funded laboratories. It springs from a rather simple insight into our own or our students' behaviors that is consistent most of the time.

Now let me give an example from educational research that is common, more expensive, less elegant, and currently not very promising, although it is still pursued with great energy by both amateur and professional researchers. I am referring to trait-treatment interaction, an area of study that has fascinated researchers for decades, reaching its zenith in the 1970s. One researcher (Goldberg, 1972) used 350 personality and other trait measures on 800 students in his study to see if any of these traits interacted with instructional methods (lecture versus self-study) and student learning outcomes (quiz versus papers). He found virtually no significant statistical interactions, but we still search endlessly for the magic technique that will maximize learning for students who differ in learning styles, ethnicity, life stage, and other individual and group differences that are easy to measure but hard to relate consistently to educational treatment.

Frankly, I confess that I am not quite sure what we would do if we found that magic technique. Would we separate or track students into homogeneous groups based on some measure of the significant learning trait? Would we direct teaching methods consistently to students' strengths, or would we conclude that to live in a complex world, students must be confronted with teaching styles that challenge their weaknesses?

Despite these reservations about the implications of the findings, as a teacher I would want to know that certain methods worked best with students with certain characteristics—not to predict who should be assigned where, but to add to my basic store of professional knowledge. Instead of speaking of applying research to practice as though it were a one-to-one relationship or formula, we should be talking more realistically about adding understanding to our base of professional knowledge. The basic purpose of classroom research is not to present or publish or report findings but to enlighten, aid understanding, and improve teaching skills.

Since almost everyone in our society equates valid

research with reporting findings, let me briefly explore the advantages and disadvantages of reporting findings. In many ways, the advantages are so obvious as to obscure the disadvantages. The obligation to report findings permits peer review, shares and advances knowledge, and forces one to examine and formulate one's own findings in some reasonably objective manner. But there are also disadvantages. The disadvantages are that present requirements for objectivity frequently result in imposing subjective impressions on objective data. Teachers, for better or worse, base their behavior more on subjective sensitivity to the nuance of the situation than on objective facts. If we have some understanding of learning styles, for example, we may respond sensitively to a student's difficulty without necessarily applying a trait-treatment interaction. We might, for example, help a student understand his or her learning style and to take effective responsibility for learning without necessarily adapting our teaching style to the multiple learning styles that occur in almost every college classroom.

Educational researchers are now beginning to move away from quantitative and statistical studies toward studies aimed at increasing understanding rather than reporting findings. Qualitative researchers, for instance, are reporting findings in narrative form—sometimes called "thick description"—in which the attempt is to give the reader who was not present an understanding of the situation. But most classroom researchers do not have time for field notes, transcriptions, and the extensive writing required in thick description. For classroom researchers, insight may be relatively quick and easy. Although discussion with colleagues helps confirm and possibly enrich understandings, a classroom researcher is neither a physicist nor an anthropologist searching for reportable findings; he or she is a professional teacher searching for understanding.

Following is a description of a classroom research project that is enormously rich in insight but scanty in reportable data. The project was carried out by Dave Nakaji, a physics teacher at Los Medanos Community College. He was interested in the question of how physics students use visualization to solve problems. He had fourteen students, too few for a valid statistical study but just enough to provide insight on how individuals solve problems. Nakaji devised some systematic procedures for observing how students go about solving physics problems. He chose a particular problem for his study because he hypothesized that for this problem, the depth of understanding was enhanced by visualization and especially by the ability to shift perceptions during the solution.

Nakaji was primarily interested in learning more about the problem-solving process, so he devised his study to provide maximum opportunity for him as a teacher to systematically observe the use of visualization. Students were given a choice of how to describe what was going on in their minds. They could draw their visualization on the blackboard, on paper, or on a flip chart. They could use verbal descriptions or hands-on materials such as modeling clay, blocks, or pipe cleaners. To make sure that he captured the nuances of individual differences, Nakaji videotaped students as they were demonstrating their visualization to him. Since videotaping is somewhat threatening to most people, he went to considerable effort to talk to students individually and in class about the videotaping procedures and to make sure students felt comfortable with the sessions.

The third step in his project involved a "cool-down" period of fifteen to twenty minutes immediately following the videotaping, during which time Nakaji engaged the student in dialogue about the process, permitting the student to fill in any gaps and allowing him to ask questions that would validate or contradict what he thought he was observing. A fourth stage involved filming the student giving feedback while he or she was reviewing the original tape; finally, Nakaji attempted to relate visualization to other characteristics of the students, such as learning style, interest, motivation, and grades.

Although Nakaji was unable to relate the visualization of these fourteen community college students to other characteristics that would constitute a breakthrough in how students use visualization in problem solving, he experienced growth as a teacher in the following ways:

1. He gained valuable insight into the use of visualization, which enabled him to know how and when to use visualization in his teaching. What he thought before his study was that poorer students failed to visualize; what he learned was that whereas good students tended to use visualization about 30 percent of the time, poor students spent an enormous range of time visualizing. All students, whether good or poor, visualize, and all have some difficulty shifting focus and point of view. Thus, he learned to teach all students to shift focus and to "zoom in and out" as they visualize the problem.
2. He experimented with a multidimensional approach to feedback from students, which increased his competence and gave him more confidence in his ability to assess and access student thinking.
3. He gained a greater understanding of the complexities and challenges associated with the craft of teaching. Nakaji drew this analogy: "Just as an accomplished poet understands the subtle nuances of how words are put together, so must the accomplished instructor understand the subtle nuances of how students put meaning together, both emotionally and intellectually."
4. Finally, he counted among his learning and appreciations the close bonding with his students that his study permitted.

Although this project was more complex and time consuming than most, it is a splendid model of classroom research—intellectually demanding, hypothesis generating, calling for systematic and insightful observation, resulting in better understanding, and rich in its applications to practice.

Classroom researchers would be foolish to eschew the quantification and scientific sophistication of educational research, but it would be equally foolish to simply emulate styles and conventions that fail to accomplish the full and unique purposes of classroom research. The purpose of classroom research is to contribute to the professionalization of teaching, to provide the knowledge, understanding, and insights that will sensitize teachers to the struggles of students to learn. Classroom research consists of any systematic enquiry designed and conducted for the purpose of increasing insight and understanding of the relationships between teaching and learning.

I have distinguished classroom research from traditional educational research, but at the same time, it is also different from lunchroom conversation about teaching, which has its merits, but these are not the same merits as those of classroom research. Classroom research is more than trading insights; it is an exploration of hypotheses specifically designed to advance knowledge of individual classroom teachers. Classroom research requires investigative skills and hard intellectual work. It is a probing, questioning, systematic pursuit of knowledge about learning and the impact of teaching on learning.

As classroom research matures as a field, there will exist a closer relationship with faculty development than with either assessment or educational research. The relationship between classroom research and faculty development is potentially strong, since they share the same focused goal—to make teaching more professional, based on understanding, insights, knowledge, and skills.

Assessment and educational research, in contrast, both have goals in addition to the ultimate improvement of teaching. For assessment, there is the obligation of accountability— to show taxpayers and educators what they are getting for their money and effort. For educational research, there is the obligation to advance scholarship and knowledge about teaching and learning through replication and validation. But for faculty development, the goal is focused on the development and growth of the teacher as a professional. Faculty development has a somewhat larger perspective than classroom research. Theoretically, if not very often in practice, faculty development includes some attention to the development of an institutional climate that supports teaching and to the personal development of faculty members in nonteaching as well as teaching roles.

Differences are most likely to appear between faculty development and classroom research in the actual program of activities and, most important, in the focus of attention. The direct goal of faculty development is to improve the performance of *teachers* by supplying information, increasing self-confidence, providing opportunities to practice teaching skills and techniques, and creating a supportive institutional climate that recognizes good teaching and is conducive to its growth. Although classroom researchers are also interested in effective teaching, the focus of classroom research is on *student* performance. Classroom research looks at student learning as a function of teaching. The premise is that it makes no difference how perfectly a teacher is teaching if students are not responding. These two approaches are really quite different. Faculty development starts with the fundamental assumption that we know what to do to improve teaching—which is not an invalid assumption. We do know a lot of things we can do to improve teaching performance.

Videotaping, for example, shows some teachers quite vividly what they are doing to distract students from learning, and student ratings have been shown similarly effective in changing some teaching behaviors. (See Cross, 1989, for a summary of these research findings.) The observation of classes by faculty colleagues or consultants from the office of teaching improvement are other ways of providing feedback to teachers on their performance. But it is important to note that in all of these activities, the *teacher's* performance is the object of study and attention. Moreover, for the most part, these popular forms of faculty development are directed more toward the removal of fairly obvious errors than toward the development of outstanding teachers who possess the basic understanding of the subtleties of their profession and its impact on learning.

Other forms of faculty development, such as lectures by authorities, newsletters, workshops, and conferences, frequently present new knowledge or offer opportunities for the development of specific teaching skills. The information provided may be on learning styles, ethnic characteristics, or adult learning preferences, for example. Opportunities for skill development frequently involve exposing teachers to a particular brand of teaching, such as mastery learning, values clarification, teaching basic writing, and the like.

The point is that in faculty development, some external observer is providing information to the teacher on how to teach more skillfully. The observer is also frequently providing feedback to the teacher on what the teacher is doing, how well he or she is doing it, and how he or she could do it better. In classroom research, the teacher is the observer rather than the observed. Classroom researchers observe students and how well they are learning.

The pathways to the improvement of teaching and learning are multiple. Assessment, educational research, and faculty development are all dedicated to the ultimate improvement of the quality of education. But if the goal of the educational reforms of the 1980s is to improve learning, then what happens when teachers meet students in college classrooms is all important.

Administrators, who once gave attention to managing their institutions, are turning now to leading their faculties and administrative colleagues in the educational task of improving the quality of education at their colleges or universities. If administrators are to have an impact on the quality of education, they will need to give some attention to the following three qualities of educational leadership:

1. Administrators must be *perceived* as interested and supportive of all efforts, on the part of anyone, to improve teaching and learning.
2. Administrators must be *knowledgeable* about what is involved in educational excellence, specifically about what makes teaching good for students and challenging and satisfying for teachers.
3. Administrators must provide appropriate *incentives* and

rewards to move people in the institution toward the overall goal of excellence in teaching and learning.

The perception of administrators as educational leaders has gained widespread acceptance in recent years, especially in institutions that pride themselves on their teaching mission. When 150 prominent community college leaders were asked to rate the importance to local colleges of the sixty-three recommendations made by the Commission on the Future of Community Colleges (1988), the two recommendations receiving top priority assignments were: (1) "Insist that good teaching is the hallmark of the community college movement, with students encouraged to be active, cooperative learners," and (2) "Make a commitment to the recruitment and retention of top quality faculty and to the professional development of these colleagues" (American Association of Community and Junior Colleges, 1988, p. 21). It seems clear from the priority given these teaching-learning recommendations that community college leaders wish to be perceived as interested in and supportive of excellence in teaching and learning.

Gaining knowledge about teaching and learning is somewhat more difficult for college administrators. Such knowledge is not routinely found in graduate-level professional preparation in the academic disciplines. Worse yet, it is not even emphasized in most doctoral programs in educational administration. Graduate programs for educational administrators, however, are now beginning to require courses in teaching and learning, and many disciplinary departments are putting new emphases on the preparation of teaching assistants for their future careers as college teachers. In addition to these efforts to prepare future generations of college leaders, workshops and institutes are adding modules on teaching and learning, and the literature and professional conferences are likewise trying to provide administrators with the necessary knowledge to lead their colleges toward quality in undergraduate education.

But whatever college administrators can do to inform

themselves about quality issues and to improve the perception that their constituents have of them as interested in and supportive of efforts to improve teaching and learning, many will still consider their primary influence to lie in devising and administering an appropriate and effective system of incentives and rewards.

Classroom research has its own built-in incentives, because the process itself is intellectually challenging, promotes discussion and recognition across disciplinary and even institutional boundaries, and enhances the status and satisfaction of teaching. There are, however, many things administrators can do to encourage classroom research, including the following:

1. Devise a promotion and tenure system that recognizes teaching performance and efforts to engage in professional activities such as classroom research.
2. Provide and support opportunities for teachers to engage in classroom research, individually, in small clusters of interested and motivated faculty, and as an important aspect of departmental improvement and evaluation.
3. Provide opportunities for teachers to increase their knowledge base and gain professional recognition through attendance at professional meetings and participation in graduate-level courses or faculty development activities emphasizing the collection and analysis of classroom research.
4. Promote local discussions of classroom research projects, affording teachers an opportunity to share designs and findings and to receive local recognition for participation in growth-enhancing professional development.

References

American Association of Community and Junior Colleges. *Teleconference Workbook. American Seminar V: Building Communities.* Washington, D.C.: American Association of Community and Junior Colleges, 1988.

Boyer, C., and others. "Assessment and Outcomes Measurement: A View from the States." *AAHE Bulletin,* Mar. 1987, pp. 8-12.

Commission on the Future of Community Colleges. *Building Communities: A Vision for a New Century.* Washington, D.C.: American Association of Community and Junior Colleges, 1988.

Cross, K. P. "In Search of Zippers." *American Association for Higher Education Bulletin,* June 1988, pp. 3-7.

Cross, K. P. *Feedback in the Classroom: Making Assessment Matter.* Washington, D.C.: American Association for Higher Education, 1989.

Cross, K. P., and Angelo, T. A. *Classroom Assessment Techniques: A Handbook for Faculty.* Ann Arbor: National Center for Research on the Improvement of Postsecondary Teaching and Learning, University of Michigan, 1988.

Eisner, E. W. *The Art of Educational Evaluation: A Personal View.* Philadelphia: Falmer Press, 1984.

El-Khawas, E. *Campus Trends, 1987.* Higher Education Panel Report no. 75. Washington, D.C.: American Council on Education, 1987.

Goldberg, L. R. "Student Personality Characteristics and Optimal College Learning Conditions: An Extensive Search for Trait-by-Treatment Interaction Effects." *Instructional Science,* 1972, *1,* 153-210.

Jones, H. E. "Experimental Studies of College Teaching: The Effect of Examinations on Permanence of Learning." *Archives of Psychology No. 68,* 1923, *10,* 5-70.

Menges, R. J. "Research on Teaching and Learning: The Relevant and the Redundant." *Review of Higher Education,* 1988, *11* (3), 259-268.

National Commission on Excellence in Education. *A Nation at Risk.* Washington, D.C.: U.S. Department of Education, 1983.

National Governors' Association. *Time for Results.* Washington, D.C.: National Governors' Association, 1986.

Turnbull, W. "Are They Learning Anything in College?" *Change,* Nov./Dec. 1985, pp. 22-26.

Wilson, R. C. "Improving Faculty Teaching: Effective Use of Student Evaluations and Consultants." *Journal of Higher Education*, 1986, 57 (2), 195-211.

CHAPTER 8

Linking Campus and State Initiatives

Arthur W. Chickering
David L. Potter

Improving teaching and learning means changing the daily behaviors and interactions of students and faculty. State rhetoric, regulations, and legislative interventions must influence institutional policies and practices in ways that modify these behaviors and interactions if we are to improve the quality of undergraduate education. We know, based on decades of research concerning college impact on student learning and development, what those basic behaviors need to be. The following principles of good practice in undergraduate education outlined by Chickering and Gamson (1987, p. 1), when acted on, strengthen motivation for learning and result in solid increases in working knowledge:

1. Encourage student-faculty contact.
2. Encourage cooperation among students.
3. Encourage active learning.
4. Give prompt feedback.
5. Emphasize time on task.
6. Communicate high expectations.
7. Respect diverse talents and ways of knowing.

Typical faculty teaching behaviors and student responses fall far short of these basic practices. Lecturing to students has long been decried, yet it is the overwhelming method of choice for college teachers. It is estimated that teachers in the average classroom spend about 80 percent of their time lecturing to students, who are attending to what is being said only about half of the time (Pollio, 1984). In addition to this evidence, the curve of what course content is forgotten by students in lecture courses is fairly steep. A generous estimate is that students forget 50 percent of lecture content within a few months (Brethower, 1977). A more devastating study finding is that even under the most favorable conditions, students retain in their heads and their notebooks no more than 42 percent of lecture content (McLeisch, 1968, p. 9). These results were obtained when students were told that they would be tested immediately following the lecture. They were permitted to use their notes, and they were given a prepared summary of the lecture. The test for immediate understanding was bad enough, but when students were tested a week later, without use of their notes, recall dropped to only 17 percent of the lecture material (Cross, 1986, pp. 3–4).

Cross's recent review of research on teaching, learning, and retention of subject matter is consistent with similar reviews carried out periodically during the last twenty years (see McClelland, 1962; Hoyt, 1965). These studies show that college grade-point averages bear little relationship to post-college success, achievement, or any other variable. McClelland (1962, p. 2) observes that "the general public—including many psychologists and most college officials—simply has been unable to believe or accept this fact. It seems so self-evident to educators that those who do well in their classes MUST go on to do better in life that they systematically have disregarded evidence to the contrary that has been accumulating for some time. Being a high school or college graduate gave one a credential that opened up certain higher-level jobs, but the poorer students in high school or college did as well in life as the top students. . . . Even for highly intellectual jobs . . . superior on-the-job performance related in no way to better grades in college."

In a later study of teaching and learning, Richardson, Fisk, and Okun (1983) documents a lack of "critical literacy," which requires clear articulation of educational goals and high levels of thinking, independence, and self-direction. Instead, classroom learning is dominated by instrumentalism, the transfer of preselected "bits" of information without analysis, synthesis, or original expression. In this situation, students become "consumers of language," and students and instructors develop complementary goals focused on the transfer of basic factual knowledge. As a result, no demands are made on students to engage in critical reading and writing activities. Richardson decries this as a "symbiotic relationship" in which faculty and students agree, through a "conspiracy of silence," to minimize effort and learning.

These perspectives inform our questions concerning the role of state legislators, executives, and statewide governing boards in improving undergraduate teaching. (We recognize that statewide boards typically are called either "governing" or "coordinating." For economy of expression we use only "governing." We recognize that, given the diversity among states, there are exceptions to the general assertions that follow. Nevertheless, most hold true for most states.) These bodies have three levers for influencing the quality of higher education:

1. *regulation*—processes for approving institutional activities, missions, budgets, and programs
2. *initiatives*—incentives or sanctions to encourage or discourage particular policies and practices
3. *rhetoric*—the influencing of the climate, attitudes, and intellectual agendas or conceptions of the role and purposes of higher education in the state.

What state-level actions reinforce behaviors and conditions that underlie the findings of Cross regarding lecturing and minimal retention, the findings of McClelland and Hoyt concerning the absence of relationship between college grades and postcollege success or well-being, and the findings of Richardson on critical literacy? Conversely, what regulatory policies and practices, what initiatives, and what kinds of agenda setting help faculty and students behave in ways more consistent with principles of good practice for undergraduate teaching and learning? And, most important, how can institutional administrators minimize the negative consequences of poor state actions and capitalize on state actions that promote good learning?

Dynamics Influencing Higher Education

Alan Ostar (American Association of State Colleges and Universities, 1988, p. 3) speaks of the "inescapable bond between state institutions and state governments," due to each institution's "relationship to regional and statewide constituents and its dependence on governmental support and encouragement." The experiences of many college and university administrators suggest that these "bonds" are often ties that bind—and chafe. A rhetoric of cooperation and unity masks tensions between autonomy and accountability (Hines, 1988, p. xxi), conflicting perceptions, and even mistrust. Under these conditions, institutional administrators, if they seek to improve teaching, need to understand the role of the state, its potential to provide leadership and resources for improvement, its capacity to constrain useful reforms, and ways they can use state offices to encourage faculty and student behaviors that strengthen learning.

The traditions and political culture of each state and its communities provide the groundwork for relationships among the key players: institutional administrators, the governor, executive agencies, the legislature, and the state higher education coordinating or governing agency. Efforts to improve teaching are encouraged or thwarted by policies and practices resulting from the interplay among these parties within existing traditions and culture.

Marked differences among these players—in perceived roles, areas of responsibility and authority, and educational priorities—lead to trouble. Evidence suggests that these differences are escalating. A recent survey, paralleling an earlier one, assessed attitudes of governors toward college and university leaders (J. Gilley, personal communication, 1989). Comparison of the surveys shows increasing hostility of governors toward university administrators; many thought their state institutions were led by incompetent administrators. When seeking advice on higher education, governors ignored college and university presidents.

Institutional administrators indicate a similar distaste for state officials, seeing them as barriers to change, dominated by financial and bureaucratic concerns, devoted to maintaining the status quo, and having insufficient commitment to achieving or sustaining quality.

Governors and governing boards assume responsibility for setting the higher education agenda and guaranteeing its quality. The governor and legislature, in consultation with the board, recognize their ability to provide resources to ensure quality and to create incentives for improvement. At this level of abstraction, there is no dispute between institutions and the state. (At a high enough level of abstraction, we all can agree about most everything!) However, when we get down to nuts-and-bolts policies and practices, conflicts emerge.

Most governors rely heavily on the knowledge and experience of executive agencies to provide continuity with preceding administrations. In turn, institutional knowledge of agency staffs figures prominently in budget formation and justification. The legislature holds the purse and enacts laws affecting institutional mission and operation. Budget politics dominate legislative processes. This makes the legislative money committees the most influential arbiters of higher education; their leaders and staffs become critically important. Although geographical dispersion of colleges and universities ensures some representation of the interests of each, legislative decision making among them is not even handed. Legislators usually are disproportionately graduates or supporters of the elite institutions of the state. They represent a multitude of other constituencies as well.

In part, governing boards exist to limit the political pressures of individual institutions on legislators and the governor. Their charge is to coordinate a system and to ensure an equitable distribution of resources. In practice, they pursue equity by establishing funding formulas. They approve changes in missions, enrollments, and new degree programs and try to discontinue "unproductive" programs. They make recommendations for operating and capital budget requests. Some boards also believe they should be agents for change through statewide advocacy for higher education, for initiatives, and for reforms. But their power to exert strong leadership often is constrained by statutory limitations or by their particular status vis-à-vis the legislative and executive branches. Many also are hampered by the uncertain vision and limited understanding of lay boards in which most members are appointed as a political reward, not for their knowledge of higher education.

During the 1980s, a number of "education governors" emerged who undertook extensive efforts to improve elementary and secondary education. Strategies to improve higher education became more targeted. These governors spoke out about mission and operation and worked behind the scenes to change leadership at selected institutions. Legislatures often responded with ongoing preoccupation with finances. Efficiency, equity, and accountability have become watchwords. At the same time, other state interest groups resisted expanding education's share of the total budget. Legislators greet with skepticism special pleadings by individual institutions, although support for particular projects can be mustered. Legislative staffs and governing boards try to minimize tough political choices among institutional pleas.

These general dynamics influencing higher education are complex indeed. The forces at work do not often give high priority to the quality of undergraduate teaching and learning but rather operate in the three major arenas of rhetoric (setting the agenda), statewide initiatives, and regulation. We turn to state policies and practices in each of these arenas and to the reactions of institutional administrators responding to them.

Rhetoric: Setting the Agenda for Improvements

Governors appoint task forces to recommend ways that higher education might better serve the state. In Virginia, for example, Governor Baliles established a Commission on the University of the Twenty-First Century, which was charged to address the skills and knowledge needed for the next several decades. The commission, comprised of legislative leaders, lay citizens, and educators from other states, is assessing the implications of economic, social, and demographic shifts underway in Virginia, recommending ways to ensure access for all state citizens who can benefit from higher education, and stimulating a review of college and university curricula, with emphasis on international studies.

Governing board directors also assume an agenda-setting leadership role. A published report by Davies (1987, pp. 20–21) recommends finding ways for the board to "leverage" its unique position within the state governmental system and urges recognition of the systemic nature of higher education.

> We have tended to deal with different aspects of the system or with individual institutions in the system as if they were unconnected, when in fact every aspect of a complex system or institution relates to every other aspect. We have created a series of distinctions within which we have applied different policies and procedures. Each policy might make sense, and each set of procedures might be coherent in itself, but they do not come together well enough as a whole. . . . We still are . . . trying to create processes in which the Council and the colleges and universities can learn within a system. One of the great ironies . . . is the extent to which institu-

tions . . . tend themselves to resist learning. . . . One of our challenges is to make the benefits of change more attractive than its costs.

This is a striking statement. It presumes that the board must seek improvements in the face of institutional intransigence and ignorance and implies that a systemic assault on quality is inimical to institutional interests. The suggestion is to take a tactical, rather than a collaborative, approach to change.

Recommendations for Presidents and Chief Academic Officers

The basic strategy for institutional administrators in responding to and working with these agenda-setting and change-agent activities by state officials is to get out in front with one's own local, regional, and intrainstitutional agendas and recommendations for change. This is especially critical for undergraduate teaching and learning when the statewide agendas emphasize research, service to business and industry, and statewide graduate programs.

Well-chosen use of the language and issues associated with statewide commissions and task forces can help drive this process. The system concept, for example, applies to the region served, the immediate location, and the institution itself. What are the particular characteristics and future needs of those systems? A statewide commission assesses the implications of economic, social, and demographic shifts underway. What do local and regional changes imply for our institution? How consistent are those implications with the ones identified by the statewide commission? What do projections concerning the ethnic and socioeconomic profiles of students in our service area imply for undergraduate education? Where do these students seek employment, and what are those job opportunities apt to be two decades hence? What is an appropriate scale for our institution? What kinds of disaggregation or decentralization might maximize a sense of community and enhance the quality of undergraduate education while responding to the growth, or the potential decline, of some of our key constituencies?

To provide an effective counterweight, the president needs to build the most powerful combination of corporate, political, organizational, and educational leaders available in the region to address these issues. These community leaders need to create clear, forward-looking agendas for the institution. They need to make their presence felt by the governor, legislature, and governing boards and to publicize and build community support for the institutional mission and image regarding undergraduate teaching and learning.

Within institutions, chief academic officers should adopt a similar strategy. The rhetoric of statewide task forces and commissions can provide the basis for initiating serious institutional agenda setting for undergraduate education. This can function to stimulate internal reviews of curricula and teaching, their appropriateness to anticipated changes in student demographics and societal needs, and their responsiveness to the shifting international circumstances students will face. The participants in this intrainstitutional agenda setting need to be broad based enough to include the formal and informal leaders of key units. This internal political group requires all the political weight it can muster if it is to have any influence on the agenda setting of the state and community government.

Statewide Initiatives

The strategy of using a portion of state funds, decoupled from enrollment-based formulas, to drive statewide initiatives has become increasingly popular. The basic approach is to fund institutions at something less than 100 percent of the guidelines and reserve any remaining funds for new initiatives. Examples of such initiatives include "centers-of-excellence" programs to boost strong programs to a higher level of visibility or for innovative projects, faculty programs that honor exceptional teachers or research scholars or promote various kinds of faculty "development," and assessment programs.

From the state's perspective, initiatives are a way to nudge the system in chosen directions—to have some leverage on institutional behavior. As one governing board member said, "Institutions are like amoebas in a culture tray. Put food in one corner and they will flow in that direction; put in acid and they will recoil in another direction." Initiatives are the food for change, at least change that lasts until another stimulus is placed elsewhere in the tray.

Recommendations for Presidents and Chief Academic Officers

College and university administrators are ambivalent about initiative funding. They do not appreciate initiatives established without their advice and counsel. They resent terms for educational improvement defined by the state and are suspicious of state intentions and hidden agendas. Realizing that political pressures tend to force a distribution of scarce initiative funds among all institutions, regardless of program quality, administrators lack confidence that relatively small sums on the margin can have a lasting effect.

Mandated student assessment is most controversial, eliciting the strongest criticism and the greatest fears. But it also gets modest endorsement from some academic leaders, who recognize that it clearly would not have been undertaken without a state mandate. At the beginning, institutions strongly resisted, but recognized, the political hazards of open opposition. They resented intrusion into their academic management and suspected governing boards would launch the program under one set of conditions and then change the terms. There were fears that pressure for easily compared results would lead to standardized testing across diverse institutions. Many of these fears persist or have been realized. But administrators can transform these tensions into creative vehicles for improvement. Each of the initiatives mentioned above can be used in ways that strengthen undergraduate teaching.

Centers-of-excellence programs offer especially powerful possibilities for strengthening undergraduate teaching. In these programs, the key strategy is to stipulate limits on the number of within-institution proposals, to set priorities that clearly focus on the quality of undergraduate education, and to use in-house reviews that apply those priorities. This strategy maximizes institutional control over what the state selects for funding. Academic officers who speak most highly of such programs play an active role, ensuring that faculty time is not wasted on proposals the institution will not support and assigning top faculty members to the task. A similar strategy can be used for faculty award or development programs. The institution can establish its own internal criteria for nomination that emphasize contributions to the quality of undergraduate teaching and set up an in-house review and application process that emphasizes teaching's importance.

Student assessment programs, despite continuing fears, also can be put to excellent use. In fact, the best protection against state movement toward standardization and superficial quantitative comparisons is to design a solid program, specifically tailored to institutional mission and local and regional agendas. The case for more general standardization will be hard to sustain when the assessment program stresses qualitative diagnostic information and not simply quantitative data; when data analyses are disaggregated by institutional program and by appropriate subcategories of students within programs; when systematic means of feeding back information to students, faculty, and administrators are implemented; and when specific improvements are identified with the results of these analyses. The limited usefulness of more abstract data sets will be more clearly apparent.

Another part of the strategy is to distinguish clearly between that information which is sent forward to the state and that which is collected and retained for local use. Carefully controlling the information that goes out and decentralizing decisions as to how best to assess particular programs or outcomes can be a strong combination. This strategy ensures broad-based institutional ownership of the program and increases the chance that information collected will be pertinent to programmatic concerns and used for diagnosis and improvement. It also protects the institution from inappropriate or superficial comparisons. Presidents and chief academic officers typically have broader knowledge of local, regional, and statewide political dynamics and therefore are best positioned to determine what information is made public. Deans, department heads, and program directors know best the kind of information that will be helpful for individual programs. Using the additional resources provided by the state for assessment in these ways can provide powerful institutional leverage for improving undergraduate teaching.

Regulation

The state's regulatory functions are the most pervasive forces influencing educational quality, creating the atmosphere and climate of education—literally, the air we breathe and the water we swim in. Regulations govern approval of institutional mission, financing, facilities, and academic programs. Like the proverbial fish in the sea, often we have become so acclimatized, so insensitive, that we are unaware how much we are shaped by these forces.

Except for a few elite universities that have accumulated endowments and that attract large federal and private research funds, public institutions are nearly totally dependent on state resources. Financial concerns dominate relations with the General Assembly and its money committees and also dominate contacts with the governor and the executive agencies. A major justification for governing boards' existence rests on planning and maintaining an effective and efficient system, with emphasis on efficiency.

Budgetary approaches are typically twofold, using standard formula based on enrollment mix and mission and recommending additional resources based on programmatic goals. Although the recent trend is toward programmatic initiative funding, the bulk of state resources continues to be allocated according to the guidelines. The guidelines standardize allocations within categories of institutional activity. Enrollments drive them, and institutions may negotiate enrollment projections with the staff for this purpose. Some categories are funded more richly than others and thus tend to weight the entire system in those directions. Graduate enrollments generate more dollars per full-time-equivalent student than upper-division courses, and upper-division students generate more dollars than lower-division students.

Faculty salaries are an example of how guidelines can reinforce categorical distinctions among institutions and maintain systemic differences in resources allocations. Average salaries for full professors at six different Virginia institutions in 1988, for example, ranged from $43,600 to $65,900, a 50 percent differential between the bottom and top. The rank order of these salaries by institution is consistent with the rank order average of *all* faculty salaries at the public colleges and universities. This ranking also mirrors the relative status of institutions within the state system, with doctoral-granting universities in the lead.

These guideline dynamics are reinforced when boards create "peer institutions" for each college and university, a set of institutions identified as having similar missions and characteristics. Once the institution and the governing board agree on the peers, the average salary of the peers becomes a benchmark toward which the state aims to improve the institution's relative standing. The hidden criteria applied in the negotiations often are the perceived relative standing of the particular institution to those institutions to which it is being compared and the actual salaries offered by potential peers. State officials may use these criteria to eliminate from peer lists institutions thought to have higher status than the particular institution and to reject institutions with exceptionally high salaries. College and university presidents may use the same criteria to advocate peers with reputations to which they aspire and to include peers who offer high salaries. The result of the process is to perpetuate salary differences among state institutions, usually with graduate research universities favored.

Governing boards also may distribute staffing guide-lines—which allocate state resources by disciplines based on different faculty to student ratios—to deans and faculty, who use these as productivity standards and for measuring faculty work load. These ratios also provide arguments for additional resources when department, school, or college enrollments exceed guideline benchmarks. Although these guidelines are used as a basis for funding, institutions are not required to distribute the resources thus generated in exact proportion to the mix used for the guidelines. Nevertheless, the guidelines do act as inhibitors, or caps, requiring administrators to make internal allocations consistent with external appropriations.

The bulk of resources generated by the guidelines come from undergraduate education, because that is where there are large enrollments. But the pressures of the funding guide-lines typically work against high-quality undergraduate edu-cation, especially given the changing demographics. The enrollment-driven character of these guidelines emphasizes quantity over quality. Their full-time-equivalent basis favors full-time students over part-time learners, who significantly outnumber on-campus residents and who will continue to grow in numbers. The formulas can weight toward graduate students and research rather than toward undergraduates and teaching and can encourage conventional pedagogy by the absence of differentiation within program categories.

The regulatory function applied to academic programs also has consequences for undergraduate teaching. Statewide boards often are empowered to approve new degree programs or to review and discontinue programs that no longer gener-ate sufficient enrollments or degrees. Through their planning responsibilities, they also can establish other programs that influence the curriculum.

In this area of program approval, governing boards have typically been reactive, responding to institutional pro-posals. But the criteria used to evaluate proposals constrain the range of potential curricular improvements. Approval is dominated by concerns with program duplication, projected enrollments, job prospects for graduates, and costs. Need must be justified in those terms, not on the basis of relationship to the total curriculum. Boards tend to be apprehensive about interdisciplinary programs and thus favor the conventional organization of knowledge. Although social problems and professional expertise seldom conform to our long-standing disciplinary categories, institutional responsiveness to these needs is constrained by this apprehension.

Governing boards are hampered in their program-approval function because no staff can carry the full range of disciplinary expertise required. Thus, the board is left with formal, rather than substantive, criteria.

Recommendations for Presidents and Chief Academic Officers

Institutional administrators do not often think that governing-board regulatory activities contribute to improving undergraduate teaching and learning. Indeed, many think that most current regulations militate against improvement. Some think that academic and budgetary responsibilities conflict; academic concerns dominate rhetoric, finances dominate policy and practice. Statewide policies and procedures are experienced as bureaucratic impediments to improvement or intrusions on the rightful academic and financial responsibilities granted to institutions and their boards. Budgetary actions are seen as subservient to purely economic considerations, emasculating institutional potentials for marshalling resources for effective innovation.

Some experienced administrators are quite specific about the impact of budgeting formulas and guidelines on undergraduate education. One chief academic officer said, "Because the formula is all student driven, we have to rob Peter to pay Paul. We have to divert resources from administration, support staff, and custodial help to have more faculty." Another chief academic officer felt more strongly, saying, "The state has produced a mentality that haunts those of us concerned with high-quality undergraduate education. When the salary formulas and institutional categories are combined, they create an orientation that destroys undergraduate education. All that counts is research. Undergraduates are cannon fodder, at the bottom of the scale. One of our faculty members is going to [a state research university] for an $8,000 increase. We could have matched that increase here, but we were not willing to because her teaching evaluations were not good. She said she doesn't like teaching here because she has to satisfy each of our students. She can go down there, set her standards, flunk 'em all out, and that's OK. She'll be rewarded for her research and grant support."

Academic administrators also are uncomfortable with the way program approval is handled. They view the procedures and criteria as bureaucratic, barriers to change, supporting of the status quo, and insensitive to institutional curricular integration.

Presidents and chief academic officers who want to give high priority to top-quality undergraduate education have tough paddling against the strong currents generated by states' funding guidelines and the normal priorities embedded in enrollment-driven funding formulas. Emphasizing excellent undergraduate teaching means establishing institutional priorities and allocating resources in ways that run directly counter to those that are symbolically and practically emphasized by the way dollars are justified and generated. In essence, it means turning those allocations on their head.

The toughest, and most important, teaching tasks are at the freshman and sophomore levels. It is here where student diversity is most extreme—in academic preparation, in motivation, and in clarity of purpose. At these levels, institutional identification; involvement with fellow students and with faculty; and clarification of career aspirations, life goals, personal identity, values, and educational plans need most attention. For most upper-division students, these matters have become more settled, for better or worse. They have more sense of direction, stronger motivation, better study habits, and more supportive relationships with faculty members and other students. Those who go on to graduate school are much more mature and advanced in all these areas. Thus, the standard funding formulas allocate the most dollars per student at the upper-division level, where they are least needed for high-quality teaching and learning.

Our recommendation is that presidents and chief academic officers tackle the difficult political and budget reallocation challenges involved in turning the system upside down. This will require clear confrontation of long-standing institutional habits and unexamined conventions and will involve political conflicts with faculty heavily invested in graduate teaching and with graduate deans and other administrative leaders. This effort will also require solid support from local board members and community leaders, who will need to become well informed about the local and regional benefits of a strong undergraduate program.

Tackling the strong formula-funding forces also will require tough negotiations with statewide governing boards so institutional discretion can be exercised and so institutional support remains constant even though local expenditures deviate sharply from the guidelines generating that support. In time, if other institutions concerned with strengthening undergraduate education act in similar ways, state budget formulas may themselves be influenced. But we can expect this level of change to move at about the speed of a glacier. One may require a geological time perspective to recognize a measurable difference.

Shifting resource allocations in the directions suggested above will make more possible many of the other recommendations made concerning setting institutional agendas and taking action that capitalizes on statewide agendas and initiatives. Such shifts also will strengthen institutional capacity to act on many of the excellent recommendations made by other authors in this volume. But in the absence of such action, in the face of pervasive pressures created by the state regulatory and funding processes and priorities, lasting results will be difficult to achieve.

Conclusion

As we review our analysis and recommendations, some general observations are worth making. On balance, our view is that the agenda-setting activities and the initiatives undertaken by state boards have been positive forces for higher education, in general, and for undergraduate education, in particular. Although there is not unanimous agreement and although there is room for significant improvement and fine tuning, the perspectives and recommendations that have come from the various governors' task forces and commissions have served the state well. These recommendations have provided a sense of direction and priorities and helped disparate forces and political interests recognize that we are, after all, interdependent. This perspective reminds us that state resources are finite and that many interests have a legitimate need for them. When institutional administrators are able to shape these perspectives to local ends, they can be useful vehicles for integrating state and institutional agendas.

Most of the initiatives undertaken also have had positive effects. Some are especially pertinent to, and helpful for, undergraduate teaching: centers of excellence, the faculty award and development programs, and student assessment programs. We think these initiatives offer opportunities for institutional administrators interested in strengthening undergraduate education.

Unfortunately, however, the state regulatory functions, as they are currently established and implemented, work powerfully against many of the recommendations made by the task forces and commissions and many of the purposes that the initiatives aim to serve. Do not misunderstand. It is not our view that the regulatory functions are unnecessary or should be eliminated. Our economic and social interdependencies require coordination and regulation. But the guidelines and assumptions through which these responsibilities are exercised are outdated and dysfunctional. Most of them were established twenty or more years ago and cry out for serious reevaluation and revision. Such reevaluations will be conceptually complex and politically challenging, to say the least. These long-standing guidelines, procedures, and assumptions have been created in the service of historically powerful prides and prejudices. Their existence through time has itself created politically strong constituencies, and they operate in a complicated system in which any changes may have unanticipated consequences. But unless these bedrock issues are tackled, efforts on the margin are unlikely to result in a system of undergraduate education that creates the competent work force and sophisticated citizenry required by our globally interdependent, information-driven world.

References

The Academy for Educational Development. "An Assessment of the Funds for Excellence Program and Subprogram on Student Recruitment and Retention." A Report to the State Council of Higher Education for Virginia, April 1988.

American Association of State Colleges and Universities. *Cooperative Leadership: The State and the University. Sharing Responsibility for the Issues Reported by the National Commission on the Role and Future of State Colleges and Universities.* Washington, D.C.: American Association of State Colleges and Universities, 1988.

Brethower, D. M. "Research in Learning Behavior: Some Implications for College Teaching." In S. C. Scholl and S. Inglis (eds.), *Teaching in Higher Education.* Columbus: Ohio Board of Regents, 1977.

Chickering, A., and Gamson, Z. *Seven Principles for Good Practice in Undergraduate Education.* Racine, Wisc.: Johnson Foundation, 1987.

Cross, K. P. "Taking Teaching Seriously." Paper presented at the annual meeting of the American Association for Higher Education, Washington, D.C., March 1986.

Davies, G. K. *Ten Years of Higher Education in Virginia. A Report to the State Council of Higher Education for Virginia.* Richmond: State Council of Higher Education for Virginia, 1987.

Hines, E. R. *Higher Education and State Governments. Renewed Partnership, Cooperation, or Competition?* ASHE-ERIC Higher Education Report no. 5. Washington, D.C.: Association for the Study of Higher Education, 1988.

Hoyt, D. P. *The Relationship Between College Grades and Adult Achievement: A Review of the Literature.* Research report no. 7. Iowa City, Iowa: American College Testing Program, 1965.

McClelland, D. C. "Testing for Competence Rather Than for Intelligence." *American Psychologist,* 1962, *28* (1), 1–15.

McLeisch, J. *The Lecture Method.* Cambridge Monographs on Teaching Methods, no. 1. Cambridge, England: Cambridge Institute of Education, 1968.

Pollio, H. R. "What Students Think About and Do in College Lecture Classes." *Teaching-Learning Issues,* no. 53. Knoxville: University of Tennessee Learning Research Center, 1984.

Richardson, R. C., Jr., Fisk, E. C., and Okun, M. A. *Literacy in the Open-Access College.* San Francisco: Jossey-Bass, 1983.

PART THREE

Making Teaching Excellence an Institutional Priority

CHAPTER 9

Ichabod Crane Dies Hard: Renewing Professional Commitments to Teaching

Harriet W. Sheridan

In 1945 although the admission of women to the Graduate School of Yale as the wartime replacement for the dominantly male population had kept the school functioning, no women were used as teaching assistants in the undergraduate classroom or, for that matter, had been appointed as faculty. Not only had we no opportunity to practice being teachers, but we also lacked a mentor to guide us into professional scholarly attitudes and values.

Our male comrades had prepared for their careers somewhat differently. They had been graders for senior professors and teaching assistants. Yet although the men had greater opportunities for classroom experience, their preparation for teaching was casual and unpredictable. Appointment en masse to the phalanx of very junior assistant professors started them off on their professional futures. Very few were kept on to succeed to the rank of associate. All of them learned the lesson of survival: scholarly promise had to become scholarly productivity. The object had been clearly defined.

What had brought us all into graduate school, and still brings today's generation of Ph.D. candidates there, was a combination of forces of which the specific encouragement of some faculty members in our undergraduate colleges and our newly educated fascination with our discipline must be deemed the most influential. The choice of graduate school was largely governed, now as then, I suspect, by any happy coincidence of nationally respected scholars with an offer of graduate financial support. I cannot remember any advice about choices of graduate schools that included mention of the teaching skills of the scholars at those schools, although some attention was given to the school's record for getting its students through the Ph.D. before the onset of senility.

And although it is true that many good teachers who are also widely known scholars do exist on graduate campuses, it is also true that many of these scholars are weak, indifferent teachers. But graduate students are brought to faculty by their enthusiastic desire to learn the mysteries of their discipline. Such students hardly need to be taught; they may be assumed to be motivated and mature enough to profit from an excellent research library and the opportunities for cutting-edge insights provided by faculty reading from their newest manuscript.

It is therefore one of the paradoxes of higher education that although skillful, committed teaching plays so large a part in encouraging undergraduates to enter advanced studies, once they arrive in graduate school, the respect accorded that influence is scant. The lions of a department are the frequently published scholars; the donkeys spend their time and energy teaching and advising large numbers of undergraduates and are rewarded in lowly fashion less for their teaching skill and more for their political contribution to the department's FTE.

Whatever lip service is paid to teaching as one of the defining criteria of the professoriate, scholarly productivity is the dominant measure, and in many institutions quantity of publications is the determinant.

This is even more the case in the sciences, where graduate students learn very early that their services are needed for assistance in grant-funded research and are actively discouraged from committing anything more than minimal time to their undergraduate classroom responsibilities. Such an attitude must carry some of the blame for the deplorable state of science teaching nationally: the "best and the brightest" are destined for research; the rest become teachers. I would suppose that instead of carping, we ought to congratulate ourselves that so many good science teachers have emerged to teach in the schools and colleges in spite of the message of the endemic reward system.

This reward system acts as a brake on the enthusiasm for teaching that graduate students arrive with. Attempts to prepare them for their stipendiary teaching functions therefore work against the grain, and strategies to enhance the teacher's role are most likely to succeed when departments, the locus of professional power, take the lead. In many universities, a significantly large portion of the conduct of the freshman curriculum has been put in the hands of graduate students. So it is at least the recognition of the political risks incurred when large numbers of increasingly sophisticated freshman consumers confront inexperienced graduate students in required introductory courses that has revived departmental senses of responsibility. Thus, more and more departments are at least providing some technical preparation and supervision for graduate students who have been saddled with staffing introductory courses in such basic fields as composition and foreign languages, courses the faculty themselves do not care to teach.

Increasing national attention is currently being focused on the teaching component of undergraduate education, a curiously muted topic in the several critiques of schools and colleges published only a short time ago. (Compare William Bennett's *To Reclaim a Legacy*, 1984, the Association of American Colleges' *Integrity in the College Curriculum*, 1985, Allan Bloom's *The Closing of the American Mind*, 1987, and others, as exceptions, the report of the National Institute of Education's Study Group on the Condition of Excellence in American Higher Education entitled *Involvement in Learning*, 1984, and Frank Newman's *Higher Education and the Ameri-*

can Resurgence, 1985, placed much more emphasis on modes of teaching.) Most of these works were inspired chiefly by nostalgia for a past in which American commerce outstripped foreign competition and the country was unified by common studies that produced common values—the Golden Age that never was. The cause of our decline was simply seen as faculty and administrative abdication of responsibility for requiring students to study what was good for them and was based on the assumption that freshmen (and sophomores) were too slack and uninformed to make the right choices voluntarily. So all students—men and women, black, Latino, Asian American, white—were to be unified in a core curriculum designed for everyone's higher needs. And this curriculum would transcend the decadent influences of rock music, pot, and unlicensed sexuality that had come to be so dominant in the American youth culture.

I need scarcely observe that such arguments in the twentieth century recapitulate the angst of previous generations of education watchers, who could at least moderate their despair at the course of higher education by founding new colleges (for example, Jefferson's disappointment with William and Mary and the establishment of the University of Virginia; or Johns Hopkins as a response to Cornell; see also Rudolph, 1977). But recent critics, scarcely giving a nod toward the substantially altered demography and the social transformations of the age, "newly" coin their solutions in changed curricular structures: core, in preference to distribution, and both far and away better than choice.

It has always seemed surprising to me that undergraduates should be held so heavily responsible for not wanting to study the influential texts of the past, such as those Bennett lists. Is the fact that they are too demanding of the reader the only explanation—or that these sources scarcely point the way toward twentieth-century employment? Yet the most popular spring course at Carleton College campus, one enrolling hundreds of students, was a course in ancient mythology taught by a professor of Greek and music. It was not an easy course, nor was it a practical one. It was taught by an excellent teacher, one who connected the past with the present, who knew his students, and who took joy in his teaching. Every campus will offer examples of this kind, suggesting that great teachers will find their students, regardless of the subject.

Whatever the effects of core curricula on undergraduates, these ventures have had at least the advantage of focusing attention on the way such courses will be taught. A well-wrought core requires that faculty from different, though related, fields work together as a team and possibly thereby demonstrate a cardinal principle of liberal education—its interconnectedness. Such collaboration must rank as a step in the direction of improved teaching, as faculty observe each other in the classroom and learn how others choose and present the materials of instruction. I think it is fair to say that feeble and unmotivated teaching of "general education" courses has had a role to play in student aversion for such courses. When faculty are bored with the content and graduate students unprepared to teach it, few undergraduates will wish to study a subject. When our weakest faculty—the so-called deadwood who are unproductive scholars and indifferent teachers—are assigned to teach giant gateway courses (prerequisites to any other course in the discipline) by their department chairs, undergraduates, graduate students, and faculty get the message. But team-taught courses cannot be maintained with weak teachers (see Allardyce, 1976), and so teaching improvement may turn out to be a result of the reinstitution of core curricula of various kinds, although it was not the prime objective of the critiques of undergraduate education.

Substantial change in the social stratification of the academy to provide greater status to the teaching function of the profession will only come about from a combination of sustained national leverage, such as is now occurring, administrative energy directed toward this end in each institution, and faculty support within their disciplinary groups. Such higher educational associations as AAC and AAHE have been devoting a portion of their annual conference to honoring the country's great teachers. AAHE, in particular, for many years has placed teaching in the center of its round of activities, including assessment conferences, issues of *Change* featuring teaching (the first report appeared in March 1976, published by Educational Change, Inc., and funded by FIPSE), and, for the past three years, ceremonies honoring teachers nominated from a variety of institutions nationwide. Since 1981 CASE has annually selected a professor of the year, whose views about teaching issues have been published in *Distinguished Teachers on Effective Teaching* (Beidler, 1986). Most recently, in a comment focused on precollegiate education, the National Board for Professional Teaching Standards (created three years ago by the Carnegie Forum on Education and the Economy) asserted that "the single most important action the nation can take to improve schools is to strengthen teaching."

The push for the improvement of college teaching has moved beyond random institutional choice and is occurring now at the state level. The New Jersey Master Faculty Program, developed by the late Joseph Katz, is expanding into an Institute for Collegiate Teaching and Learning, for which the University of Wisconsin's systemwide Faculty College serves as one model. The State System of Higher Education of Pennsylvania has just begun a Summer Academy for the Advancement of Teaching. Other state systems have either initiated such programs recently or are contemplating doing so. All of this is cheering news. As recognition spreads across the country of the criticalness of skilled teaching to the success of any curricular program, on whatever level, summer institutes, centers for instructional development, "teacher of the year" awards and other marks of favor will proliferate.

However, radical change of the social structure of the profession will not come easy. The ascendancy of specialized learning in the last century reduced our sense of responsibility for undergraduate education. Encouraged by such enterprising college presidents as Charles William Eliot of Harvard, Andrew Dickson White of Cornell, and Daniel Coit Gilman of Johns Hopkins, the professionalization of the academic function through scholarly research was perceived as a helpful defense of intellectual values in a mass society "that threatened to withhold deference from even the highest values" (Thomas L. Haskell, in Bouwsma, 1985, p. 11). In the founding of Johns Hopkins, the nation took as its model the German university's emphasis on scholarship and graduate study.

As a by-product of this focus, although it is likely that any faculty member who is required to teach undergraduates would prefer to be regarded by them as a good teacher, very few will reallocate their energies in order to spend more of themselves in teaching.

Moreover, faculty harbor the deep suspicion that the subject of teaching is "soft" and anecdotal, therefore unverifiable or unassessable. The clownish image of Ichabod Crane hovers spectrally in the wings of the academic profession on all levels. "Teachers in this country have always had an image problem," Edward B. Fiske remarked in a recent column in the *New York Times* (July 19, 1989, p. B6), supporting this assertion by citing a report in *The Maryland Journal* of 1776: "A ship [has] arrived in Baltimore from Belfast and Cork with a cargo that included 'various Irish commodities, among which are beef, pork, potatoes and schoolmasters.' "

At the center of faculty suspicion is the conviction that scholarship not only can be assessed objectively by referees but also endures as a lasting contribution to our store of knowledge. However, a whole body of skeptical responses has accrued around the assessment of teaching. "Popular" teachers are easy teachers, and/or they are mere entertainers— lightweights. Student evaluations are typically affected by the teacher's personality. Highly rated colleagues pander to students' desire for undemanding courses and easy grades. Teaching evaluations are the result of transitory vogue among immature students, who lack the wisdom to judge true value in the long run. When students are critical, it is because youth is hard to please or is too shallow to perceive underlying structures and values. Poor ratings reflect teaching style, and are largely the result of lecturing inadequacies rather than any more fundamental lack. Peer evaluations of teaching are

time consuming, unreliable, unfocused, and generally sporadic. And, in any case, teaching is an art dependent for its
success on the unique personal characteristics of individuals.
It cannot, therefore, be objectively measured or replicated.
(See Robert Boice and Jim Turner, "Helping Faculty Recognize Myths About Teaching Evaluations," cited in Cross,
1989.)

These attitudes are widespread on campuses and
undoubtedly reflect some experienced truth. Popular teachers
are often so because of factors of personality or laxity. Peer
evaluation can be embarrassed or threatening or ill informed.
The measurement of the contribution skillful teaching makes
to the well-being of society, the counterpart of scholarship's
contribution to knowledge, is undefined and, consequently,
unregarded. Yet the pages of histories of universities are filled
with accounts of great teachers (and even of those who were
tarred and feathered by irate students), only rarely of great
scholars. And even today, at colleges and universities around
the country, ritualistic alumni visits are marked by nostalgic
reminiscences about teachers who made a difference, and
chairs are endowed with alumni or parental funds to honor
the great teachers of undergraduate years.

Scholars rightly honor scholars. They receive federal
and foundation grants, promotions and endowed chairs, competitive salaries, and the homage of their colleagues. Undergraduates, for their part, scarcely distinguish between the
most illustrious of scholars and the lowliest of graduate student section leaders: anyone who stands in front of the room
is professor. And secular society at large, although it may
seek the services of well-credentialed faculty for immediate
practical needs (managing polls of public opinion, for example, or testifying about corporate mismanagement of various
kinds, or serving on government's economic councils), on the
whole remains ignorant of the status differentiation of the
academy.

The deadliest devaluation of the teaching role lies in
the widespread belief, shared by administrators as well as faculty, that scholarship keeps the mind supple whereas teaching

deadens and rigidifies. The intellectual vitality that scholarly research creates is automatically assumed to express itself in vigorous, stimulating teaching. The reverse is only occasionally allowed. To argue that specialized research keeps the mind sharp and therefore benefits students is to express one of the pieties of higher education. But to argue that skillful teaching provides its own kind of intellectual stimulus, and that the classroom frequently generates fresh insights into a field or even suggestions about research still to be done, is to make an infrequent case. A faculty member who faces a class of premed students bored and annoyed at being forced to study the required physics course, no matter how successful his own research program may be, will find a different kind of intellectual stimulus, no less vigorous and rewarding, in the conquest of his students' smug disinclination for seemingly irrelevant fields.

And a faculty member who intends to develop student understanding of the values of an eighth-century epic, in a language no longer intelligible as English, must exercise a sharpened judgment and a fastidious discrimination to avoid patronizing both *Beowulf,* a poem about a mighty hero of a fifth-century culture, and its reluctant readers (Superman and Rambo, get ye hence!).

Of course, classroom triumphs are ephemeral. Who is on the spot to note them except callow youth with their unformed judgments? Nothing tangible remains for referees to appraise objectively. The intellectual stimulation shared by faculty and students remains within the classroom walls.

If the balance of power is ever to be shifted to an equivalence between the values placed on disciplinary scholarship and on teaching, administrators must take on a critical role, ever mindful of the risks to one's professional future that may adhere to any role that seems in the eyes of the faculty to be advancing skillful teaching to a shared prominence with published scholarship. College presidents who are indiscreet enough to override tenure decisions in favor of the excellent, if only modestly published, teacher, will lose their faculty's confidence: their careers will vanish with the daylily. But, in spite of the penalties, an important job is waiting to be done, supported increasingly by the nation's sense that something is seriously awry in academe, and administrators, joined by faculty, must do it.

It will not do merely to establish instructional development centers of various kinds, directed by faculty from departments of education or by specially appointed administrators. Important and useful as such centers may be, their role is typically to provide assistance for the technological components of skillful teaching, such as the development of techniques of leading a discussion or a seminar, constructing examinations, asking questions, and so on. Videotaping opportunities, and trained observers who may be invited into one's classroom, are generally made available for faculty who seek these aids. Not all faculty, by any means, do seek such aids. They are least frequently sought by faculty who most need them.

The presence on campuses of centers of instructional development may be augmented by formal assessment services, which arrange for the distribution of student course evaluation questionnaires and which tally these in some formulaic way, frequently with restricted circulation. Repeated criticisms on such questionnaires may be the goad that stirs faculty to seek the services of the center. And certainly the presence of such a center gives testimony to a good-faith effort on the part of an institution to raise its level of teaching performance.

But centers do not fundamentally affect the social status of teaching in the academic hierarchy. They merely announce that teaching techniques can be learned, which is, of course, the case, without enhancing the prestige of the function. Only a sweeping review of the modes by which teaching is refereed, a review that is companion to the current national assessment movement but that is indigenous to the faculty of a campus, will lead to enhancement.

As a further influence on improving the status of teaching within the professoriate, formal research into teaching and learning, which is conducted by faculty within all disciplines, and which may produce results unique to a specific discipline, needs its own definition and criteria of excellence as another form of respectable scholarship. Such studies, when published, should be given critiques comparable to disciplinary publications in their objectivity and the credentials of their referees (see Cross and Angelo, 1988). Research that makes a contribution to improved student learning of a field, and is adequately validated by standardized processes, will be weighted as heavily as disciplinary research in tenure and promotion decisions when administrators and respected faculty join together to insist on this parity. Only when research into the teaching of a field comes to be esteemed as valid scholarship, when publication in *College English* is regarded with the same favor as publication in *PMLA*, or in the *Journal of Chemical Education* vis-à-vis the *Journal of the American Chemical Society*, can a fundamental change of values be said to be taking place.

The means by which teaching is reviewed and its value to a campus is confirmed and enhanced is a task for administrative initiative. The aim is to multiply perspectives and thereby to reduce the list toward subjectivity that a single mode might be suspected of producing. Such a review should include the following components:

1. Carefully structured departmental peer reviews, conducted over a period of time, for which the reviewers must be trained to observe the fulfillment of the department's objectives as well as institutional needs that have been previously identified and agreed on.
2. The recommendation of a departmental mentor, a master teacher, who has been given the responsibility of advising and consulting with a colleague about teaching issues, and engaging in team teaching whenever possible.
3. Regular solicitation of views of alumni about the teaching skills of their undergraduate faculty. These views will be found in a high degree of conformity with those of current undergraduates, with occasional interesting exceptions.

4. Administrative sponsorship of faculty teaching presentations to a wide range of campus faculty. Such presentations may be on an individual's research project or on teaching issues. The quality of the lecture is thereby displayed before a heterogeneous group of colleagues.

In concert with strengthening the perception of the importance of teaching by making it both more visible to the community and more substantially evaluated, administrators should support a series of campuswide panels on the relationship between what is known and what is taught. An explanation of the changes in requirements from one student generation to the next, plumbing the mysteries of the course catalogue, might allay suspicion that curricula are like the wind that bloweth where it listeth. Did the reduction of requirements in the 1960s really produce a throw-away generation, the Yuppies? Is it unrealistic to ask science faculty to teach serious and respectable courses in their fields to prospective citizens and consumers rather than specialists? (The same question should be asked of humanists and social scientists.) A faculty committee should be charged with developing several topics concerned with educational issues for discussion each year. Off-campus spokespersons should be invited to join in presentations about these issues. A videotape library of master teachers in action can be made readily available for borrowing by faculty.

The specific preparation of graduate teaching assistants and the initiation of new faculty should include demonstrations of student learning differences to which all faculty should be invited. However these are sponsored, whether by a center or by a series of discussions supported by an administrator, they should identify differences originating in gender, race, and ethnic background as well as in such disabilities as dyslexia. These presentations should become a repeated part of a series devoted to teaching issues.

A carefully constructed system of faculty development in the realm of student learning, the work of Joseph Katz and Mildred Henry, which advocates a sensitive application of the

"Omnibus Personality Inventory," is described in *Turning Professors into Teachers* (1988). The growing body of research into the differences in styles of learning between men and women (see the seminal work of William Perry and Carol Gilligan), and the impact of racism, both conscious and unintended (see Cones, Noonan, and Janha, 1983), a particularly critical subject now on the nation's campuses, is known to most administrators and to few faculty. Such research is typically regarded as the domain of faculty in education, rather than in such applied disciplines as mathematics, history, or philosophy. Getting it applied in the classroom will be more likely to occur in an environment in which teaching considerations have been given more prominence institutionally.

Increasingly, signs are visible that faculty, grown older, who have taught successfully in the past, feel the need for help with new generations of students. "They don't care about anything," a physics professor lamented at a recent conference. "What used to get my students excited leaves my classes nowadays bored and restless."

Changes in the academic job market that are now occurring have made the rewards of helping undergraduates learn one's field well, and possibly go on to graduate study (which in the 1960s was dismissed for its irrelevancy and in the 1970s and early 1980s for its impracticality), seem much more realistic and have added to the motivation for skilled and devoted teaching.

If it is true that many faculty quietly wish to be able to devote more of their time and energy to the teaching role but are kept from doing so by the priority placed on published disciplinary research by their institutions (see Boyer, 1987, and Seldin, this volume), then the cure for this characteristic imbalance of professorial functions is at hand. Administrators have it within their competence to provide incentives for faculty to take up educational responsibilities earlier generations routinely performed within their disciplinary courses as teachers of writing and analytical reading and critical thinking. The categorical imperative of "content coverage" that so many faculty claim binds them to lecture with scarcely a pause serves as a preventive to students' active integration of knowledge and understanding of meaning and succeeds in doing little else than filling notebooks. Although I am bemused by the perception of a need to provide separate critical thinking courses, surely an indictment of defect in general education curricula (see Browne and Keeley, 1989), yet this latest educational movement is a sign of a renewed definition of professorial function and the determination to ensure that students are not being educationally shortchanged as they accumulate their credits. But surely departments could be asked to review and identify honestly such of their courses as emphasize vital intellectual skills (to be noted in catalogue copy) and to conduct colloquia to prepare their faculty to teach them.

Every campus generates its own climate, and wise and courageous administrators will know how to direct the winds of change to the advancement of undergraduate teaching. Not for many years have we felt this need. As the decades have passed, we have sought to explain educational losses by viewing and reviewing a procession of curricular changes and programs, paracolleges and honors programs, experiential learning, competency-based objectives, instruction via computer, revised distribution and renegotiated core, and so forth. But criticisms of higher education's performance have now shifted opportunely to an intense focus on a professionally neglected, even disparaged function, teaching. The valuable contributions of scholars who also teach undergraduates to the prestige of an institution and the betterment of society need not be lessened by recognition of the equality of value to the institution and society provided by teachers who also do research, research more broadly defined than has thus far been allowed. Our institutions are neither Bell Laboratory Research Facilities nor remedial camps staffed by jolly counselors. They are dynamic centers of knowledge and energy, a chief source for the preparation of the generations of citizens who represent the future of this nation. Their function is too critical to be warped by one professorial function to the disadvantage of another. The means to right this imbalance are evident and available and do not demand that we surrender our faith in the importance of a faculty of scholars who create new knowledge and train their successors after the continental model, only that we also recognize, with appropriate signs of our esteem, the faculty who teach with vitality and purposefulness on our native ground.

References

Allardyce, G. "The Rise and Fall of the Western Civilization Course." *American Historical Review,* 1976, "Forum," 695–725.

Association of American Colleges. *Integrity in the College Curriculum.* Washington, D.C.: Association of American Colleges, 1985.

Beidler, P. G. (ed.). *Distinguished Teachers on Effective Teaching.* New Directions for Teaching and Learning, no. 28. San Francisco: Jossey-Bass, 1986.

Bennett, W. *To Reclaim a Legacy.* A report on the humanities in higher education. Washington, D.C.: National Endowment for the Humanities, 1984.

Bloom, A. *The Closing of the American Mind.* New York: Simon & Schuster, 1987.

Bouwsma, W. J. "Specialization and Professionalism within the University; Specialization, Departmentalization and the Humanities." American Council of Learned Societies *Newsletter,* 1985 (3, 4), 11.

Boyer, E. L. *College: The Undergraduate Experience in America.* New York: Harper & Row, 1987.

Browne, M. N., and Keeley, S. M. "The Need for Critical Thinking Courses." In *The Bulletin.* Cape Girardeau: Intellectual Skills Development Association, Southeast Missouri University, 1989.

Cones, J. H., III, Noonan, J. F., Janha, D. (eds.). *Teaching Minority Students.* New Directions for Teaching and Learning, no. 16. San Francisco: Jossey-Bass, 1983.

Cross, A. "Thoughts on Evaluation." In *The Center.* Boone, N.C.: Faculty Development and Institutional Services Center of Appalachian State University, 1989.

Cross, K. P., and Angelo, T. A. *Classroom Assessment Techniques. A Handbook for Faculty.* Ann Arbor: National Center for Research to Improve Postsecondary Teaching and Learning, University of Michigan, 1988.

Fiske, E. B. "Teachers May No Longer Be Lumped With Potatoes, But an Image Problem Persists." *New York Times,* July 19, 1989, p. B6.

Katz, J., and Henry, M. *Turning Professors into Teachers.* New York: ACE/Macmillan, 1988.

National Institute of Education, Study Group on the Condition of Excellence in American Higher Education. *Involvement in Learning.* Washington, D.C.: National Institute of Education, 1984.

Newman, F. *Higher Education and the American Resurgence.* Princeton, N.J.: Carnegie Foundation for the Advancement of Teaching, 1985.

Rudolph, F. *Curriculum: A History of the American Undergraduate Course of Study Since 1636.* The Carnegie Foundation for the Advancement of Teaching: San Francisco: Jossey-Bass, 1977.

CHAPTER 10

Leadership in Action: A Campuswide Effort to Strengthen Teaching

Robert H. McCabe
Mardee S. Jenrette

Teaching and learning are at the core of any educational institution; they are its reason for being. It follows, then, that every activity an institution engages in affects its teaching-and-learning efforts and that any effort to improve teaching and learning must engage the entire institution.

The case of Miami-Dade Community College (M-DCC) is offered to illustrate the progression from accepting the challenge to improve teaching quality to implementing sweeping changes in institutional practices. The kinds of institutional support and follow-through that are needed and a workable process to achieve success are detailed.

The Start: President's Perspective

The letter from the graduating student was like so many others the president had been pleased to receive, praising the college and crediting it with her success. But, also like so many others, the real message was about particular faculty members who had gone out of their way to help her, who had believed in her and had inspired her. She wrote that when she first came, she was not certain she could make it. It had been ten years since she had been a mediocre high school student. She was working and had a family. But people at the college who cared had given her confidence, and she felt it had made the difference. That letter reminded the president how obvious it is, in an institution like Miami-Dade, that excellence is dependent on caring faculty who give of their time freely and support students. Yet it was equally obvious that this simple truth was not being acted on. The institution did not seem to be supporting and rewarding faculty behavior that really makes a difference for students.

That 1985 letter acted like a magnet, attracting other matters relating to faculty as an essential resource that had been on the president's mind for the past year. This college, like so many other institutions, was about to experience significant faculty turnover. Those faculty who had been hired in the 1960s, who were committed to providing educational opportunities to all who wanted to learn, would be leaving. Would the college also lose the extensive teaching-and-learning expertise those faculty had developed?

He had also been wondering why college faculty seem to eschew the wealth of research about adult learning that has been amassed over the last twenty years. Institutions do not seem to discourage this practice, hiring teachers based on expertise in a field with little attention to their skills in facilitating the most complex activity—learning. One would never hire a heart surgeon who had tremendous knowledge about the heart but had never held a scalpel. Like other professionals, college teachers should stand on the shoulders of those who come before, profiting from practical experience as well as a sound research base. Each generation should advance the profession beyond the achievements of its predecessors.

Without doubt, there has been a decline in the status of teaching that has occurred with the expansion of higher education and the increasing number of students and teachers. College faculty are simply not held in the same high regard that they were twenty years ago, and the compensation is inappropriate for the preparation and skills required by the profession. In a public television series about education in America, President Bush commented that teachers will never be paid like other professionals, that people go into teaching because of a high calling and principally look for nonmonetary rewards. He is wrong, and that commonly held concept needs to be changed. The days when college faculty lived in garrets and made great personal sacrifice in order to continue in teaching are gone.

Certainly teaching may bring great personal satisfaction, but faculty also expect to be able to support their families in the same manner as other professionals. Particularly true in urban areas such as Miami is the increasing number of faculty holding part-time jobs to supplement income. In some cases, especially for those with skills in high demand, one wonders if they have enough energy left for teaching.

At the 1986 American Association of Higher Education annual meeting, K. Patricia Cross spoke on classroom research. It occurred to the president that this concept might play a key role in an effort to address these issues that had become serious concerns to him. On the plane back to Miami from that conference, he wrote a draft proposal that was the beginning of the teaching-learning reform currently underway at Miami-Dade. Almost ten years before the college had pioneered in establishing a series of systems with the objective of giving good advice to students and placing them in the best situation for academic success. Now it was time to look at the teaching-learning environment itself. The college would attempt systematically to change the way that it does business in order to raise the status of teaching; improve teaching and learning at the college; relate all of the reward systems to classroom performance; and change the decision-making process such that the first priority is teaching, learning, and the classroom environment.

The Plan

Deciding to take improving teaching and learning from concept to implementation plan was an important step. Fully committing the college to this direction would require a long period of planning and substantial involvement by faculty and administrative leadership. Further, the result would likely be significant systemic change in institutional operations. Everyone at the college would feel the impact directly.

The plan as initially conceived turned out to have a serious omission. We made a logical and common mistake: we thought that institutionwide improvements in teaching and learning could be made simply by working with teaching faculty and concentrating on their efforts inside the classroom. Fortunately, based on our previous experience with the student systems reform, we understood that the initial concept would be shaped as more and more people became involved. We understood that what emerged, while moving toward the same goals, might be very different from what originally had been conceived. In this case, a story about chalk provided the insight that improving teaching and learning was going to necessitate changing administrative behavior as well as faculty behavior. The vice-president for the north campus addressed a frustration that many faculty had communicated to him; the administration and the institution's bureaucracy appeared not to give faculty needs high priority, yet at the same time they expected faculty to do excellent jobs. The illustration he offered was chalk, chalk of a type the purchasing department bought because it came at the best price, even though every teacher knew it was too hard to write well with. Believing there was no remedy available through the system, some conscientious faculty were buying good chalk and carrying it around in their pockets to use in the classroom. Defective lightbulb stories and others followed the chalk tale, with the discussion resulting in a significantly expanded scope for the Teaching-Learning Project.

The chalk incident reinforced the value of using research as a base for decisions. Thus, as we set up the project, it was understood that staff from institutional research would be available to assist in gathering data. No matter how obvious a particular recommendation might seem to those about to present it, it would not be made without providing opportunity for input, feedback, and analysis of returns on surveys or questionnaires.

In part to support the prior decision, a commitment also had to be made to take as long as necessary to permit substantial numbers of persons in the college to be brought into the process. The plan would have to provide for significant involvement and opportunity for a great deal of feedback. The section dealing with faculty advancement—that is, tenure decisions, evaluation, promotion, and awarding of endowed teaching chairs—would go to a referendum of the full faculty. The referendum decision was not made lightly; knowing that most people resist change, several years of work could come to naught if there was not a positive vote. Although the strategy was risky and would pose a real challenge to the process, we believed the decision was essential to achieve meaningful results.

The Implementation Process

In the spring of 1986, a month after the AAHE annual conference, the president introduced the broad concept of the Teaching-Learning Project to leadership from all quarters of the college at an off-campus luncheon meeting. With the objective of beginning the work in the fall of 1986, a budget was established using college staff and program development funds and monies from the Mitchell Wolfson, Sr., Foundation. A full-time director and a twenty-six-member steering committee were appointed. Each of the four campus faculty senates nominated faculty to serve on the steering committee, and they were joined by administrative appointees. Periodically persons with expertise who were not otherwise involved in the process would be brought in to review our work and interact with us about it. A day-long kick-off session was held in the fall of 1986 with the steering committee and eight invitees who represented other community colleges and universities.

The work began slowly in late fall and in earnest in the winter of 1987. By then it was clear that specific tasks would have to be assigned to subcommittees if work was to be productive. Each subcommittee would be chaired by a faculty member of the steering committee, and membership would be expanded to broaden the base of direct involvement. To communicate the importance of the effort and to recognize the time it would take, faculty would be granted released time to participate. By that winter, more than fifty faculty had released time and were serving on subcommittees. The initial set of four subcommittees was charged to examine specific issues: the shared values concerning teaching and learning at the college; fundamental characteristics that could define faculty excellence related to effective teaching and learning; services that support the teaching-learning environment itself; and those processes that result in effective recruitment, selection, and integration of new faculty into the college. Each of the subcommittees would begin work by exploring relevant research and by surveying appropriate constituencies of the college community: faculty, staff, and administrators in all instances and, in the case of faculty excellence, students and graduates as well.

We recognized there would be times when these strategies would be inadequate. For very complex or sensitive issues, more intense effort and concentration might be needed. For those matters, off-campus retreats would be planned as supplementary activities. The feedback from all sources would be analyzed, and work would be refined and finally presented to appropriate college bodies including the board of trustees. As subcommittees completed their tasks, new ones would take their place. Succeeding recommendations would be built on the work of those who had come before.

By the second year, a values document and statement of faculty excellence had been adopted. Three new subcommittees were formed, bringing an additional twenty faculty directly into the Teaching-Learning Project. Two of the new groups were to deal directly with faculty skill building. The first would investigate classroom feedback as a technique to improve teaching and learning, a concept stemming directly from Pat Cross's work on classroom research. The second would explore factors in addition to academic preparation that have an impact on student performance (for example, learning styles, cultural background) and the implications they might have for teaching strategies. The third subcommittee, focusing on faculty advancement, would make recommendations related to faculty evaluation and the institutional reward system (including tenure, promotion, and endowed teaching chairs), such that efforts to improve teaching and learning would be supported and recognized.

By the fall of 1988 some of the recommendations were ready to be put in place. During that academic year, too, the last of the issues to be addressed by the project were identified, and subcommittees were charged with topics. Matters relating to the use of adjunct faculty, the role of nonclassroom faculty (for example, counselors and librarians), the administrator's role in supporting teachers, and excellence in the support staff role were all on the agenda. As important as the issues themselves were, the new subcommittees brought more than forty new participants into the Teaching-Learning Project. The number of individuals directly involved in making recommendation on teaching and learning at Miami-Dade had exceeded 100.

Key Outcomes

Although it may be true that every activity an institution engages in affects its teaching-and-learning efforts, the further from the classroom often the less obvious the connection. The connection is there, however, and it follows that any planned change in one area will automatically bring change in others. From the beginning we held this concept. We knew it would be important to create subcommittees that would take an institutionwide view and that they would have to be created in logical order so that the work of each might form a strong base for the next. Pieces would have to fit together and recommendations would need to be integrated. Not to do so would leave weak links that might mean that no matter how good our intentions, benefits might not ever reach students.

Understanding something as a concept and dealing with its manifestations are not the same thing. The further along we got, the more complex things became. Subcommittees not only had to check with constituents, they also had to keep referring to the work of other subcommittees. Sometimes one piece of work got ahead of one it was supposed to follow. Other times individuals to be interviewed balked, saying they felt "surveyed to death." Diplomatic coaxing became a very important skill for committee members.

Despite the occasional rough going, unexpected developments, and temporary setbacks, progress on the Teaching-Learning Project has been steady and within the originally projected time frame. The first concrete outcome was an institutional values document adopted by the district board of trustees in December 1987. All faculty, staff, and administrators and a sample of students participated in a year-long process of surveying and consensus building, an effort that yielded the following shared values concerning teaching and learning at the college.

Miami-Dade Community College values:

- Learning
- Change to meet educational needs and to improve learning
- Access while maintaining quality
- Diversity in order to broaden understanding and learning
- Individuals
- A systematic approach to decision making
- Its partnership with the community

Probably as important as the values themselves were supporting statements illustrating ways in which the college makes its values operational. Those supporting statements provide a means for the Board of Trustees to gauge administrative effectiveness in supporting what we say we value.

The statement of faculty excellence, which clearly reflected the values adopted a few months before, was the next piece to follow. It went before the Board in October

1988. That substantial agreement could be reached among faculty, administrators, and students on a core set of qualities and characteristics of excellent faculty at Miami-Dade is quite remarkable. Two rounds of written surveys, small-group feedback sessions, and a two-day off-campus retreat of seventy college persons and nine outside experts took place before a final draft was prepared. The repeated invitations to contribute and then critique the subcommittee's work helped develop the necessary support for the final product.

In the statement, the descriptors of faculty excellence fall into four categories: motivation and ability to motivate others, interpersonal skills, knowledge base, and skill at applying this knowledge. The statement of faculty excellence was distributed throughout the college in detailed narrative format; the summary that follows provides a sense of the focus and scope of that document.

A. *Motivation.* Excellent faculty members at Miami-Dade Community College, whether classroom teachers, librarians, counselors, or serving in any other faculty capacity:
   1. Are enthusiastic about their work.
   2. Set challenging individual and collective performance goals for themselves.
   3. Set challenging performance goals for students.
   4. Are committed to education as a profession.
   5. Project a positive attitude about students' ability to learn.
   6. Display behavior consistent with professional ethics.
   7. Regard students as individuals operating in a broader perspective beyond the classroom.
B. *Interpersonal Skills.* Excellent faculty members at Miami-Dade Community College, whether classroom teachers, librarians, counselors, or serving in any other capacity:
   1. Treat all individuals with respect.
   2. Respect diverse talents.
   3. Work collaboratively with colleagues.
   4. Are available to students.
   5. Listen attentively to what students say.

    6. Are responsive to student needs.

    7. Are fair in their evaluations of student progress.

    8. Present ideas clearly.

    9. Create a climate that is conducive to learning.

C. *Knowledge Base.* Excellent faculty members at Miami-Dade Community College, whether classroom teachers, librarians, counselors, or serving in any other capacity:

    1. Are knowledgeable about their work areas and disciplines.

    2. Are knowledgeable about how students learn.

    3. Integrate current subject matter into their work.

    4. Provide perspectives that include a respect for diverse views.

    5. Do their work in a well-prepared and well-organized manner.

D. *Application of Knowledge Base.* Excellent faculty members at Miami-Dade Community College, whether classroom teachers, librarians, counselors, or serving in any other capacity:

    1. Provide students with alternative ways of learning.

    2. Stimulate intellectual curiosity.

    3. Encourage independent thinking.

    4. Encourage students to be analytical listeners.

    5. Provide cooperative learning opportunities for students.

    6. Give constructive feedback promptly to students.

    7. Give consideration to feedback from students and others.

    8. Provide clear and substantial evidence that students have learned.

The values document and statement of faculty excellence, taken together, form a firm foundation on which to build the rest of the work of the project. They help, for instance, to create a profile of an individual who would be a desirable addition to the faculty. Knowing that all those involved in the hiring process are carrying a similar picture makes for a smoother search and screening process. As important, these documents help communicate the philosophy, culture, and expectations of Miami-Dade. Selection is a mutual process; a candidate selects a college, and the college selects the candidate.

For those who eventually become faculty, the documents form the orientation core. A preservice orientation for new faculty was offered for the first time in the fall of 1988. Its agenda grew, in part, out of a new faculty subcommittee survey of recent hires in which 72 percent of those responding recommended a planned orientation program. In fact "faculty orientation" was the most frequent response to the question "What additional support was needed during the first year of employment?" As piloted in 1988, the five-day new faculty orientation is comprised of a two-day collegewide program during which the president and district administration welcome the new faculty members; values, mission, priorities are highlighted; personnel matters are discussed; and faculty governance is described. The following three days are campus based, the last two being spent with an assigned mentor. The first orientation taught us to be wary of information overload, to build in more discussion time, and to invite "old" new faculty to present to new faculty. However, participant comments such as "The values of Miami-Dade Community College came through loud and clear!" and "The information given for the most part was essential for a new faculty member," and "The most important aspect for me was a sense of pride and belonging to a progressive school" told us we were on the right track. During the new faculty member's first year, sessions will continue on a monthly basis to provide orientation to campus learning resources, academic computing, campus procedures, professional growth opportunities, academic advisement, and special programs for special student populations, among others.

The values document will be a basis for the development of service area and administrative evaluations, key recommendations of the teaching-learning environment subcommittee. The research of this group made it clear that although excellent teaching is, of course, a key ingredient in positive student outcomes, it is not enough. It is only with excellent service in support of classrooms that ranges from audiovisual, custodial, plant maintenance, and duplicating and purchasing to assessment and advisement that the highest-quality environment can be created to facilitate teaching and encourage learning. Recommendations call for goals related to teaching and learning to be set by all service areas in collaboration with faculty. Evaluation of service will include feedback from deliverers and users of the service. Also to improve the teaching-learning environment, the college adopted a "hotel strategy" in 1989. The hotel analogy has been useful. Surveys of colleagues revealed a probable explanation of why repairs in classrooms seem rarely to be made: faculty, like hotel guests, are constantly passing through an assigned room. They may see problems but assume that someone else must be responsible for their resolution. The analogy can be carried further. A good hotel does not wait for an irate guest to report a lack of soap or a broken towel rack; it sends a housekeeper with a checklist around daily to each room. So Miami-Dade will shift resources in order to send a housekeeper around with a list of standards for classrooms and laboratories. We call this our Marriott Plan.

A number of outcomes have been realized regarding initial and ongoing faculty development and support. Every subcommittee recommended training to help affected groups make the transition to the new procedures being proposed and the new behaviors those procedures would require. With the statement of faculty excellence setting the standard, direction for professional development program planning becomes clear.

The presidents of Miami-Dade and the University of Miami paved the way for project subcommittees to work collaboratively with faculty from the university. Two graduate courses in teaching and learning were developed and were offered for the first time in the 1988 academic year. The "Research in the Classroom" course helps faculty hone skills in the design of assessment techniques. The intent is for faculty to be able to analyze the learning going on in their courses and to adjust their teaching strategies appropriately to enhance learning. The course "Effective Teaching and Learning" focuses more heavily on a repertoire of teaching strategies and the relative effectiveness of each with diverse student populations. Learning preferences, student motivation, and cultural considerations are among the topics addressed. We believe strongly enough in the merit of these courses to have made them mandatory (with the college paying tuition) for all new faculty as a condition for tenure application. No matter how valuable, however, one course taken one time does not "fix" a teacher for an entire career. Along with formal course offerings, both subcommittees recommended that each campus be given the resources to support an ongoing Teaching-Learning Center. The centers were in place for fall 1989.

Driving all program components in which changes in faculty behavior will be called for is a set of outcomes that fall under the umbrella of faculty advancement. One can hope faculty will perform in accordance with the qualities of excellence. One can ensure it to some degree by instituting an annual performance review and by making performance the basis for granting tenure and promotion in academic rank. In April 1989 fifteen months of work by the faculty advancement subcommittee was brought to a faculty referendum. Of those eligible, 74 percent voted by a two-to-one-margin to accept new policies regarding faculty advancement.

The process leading to the referendum was characterized by faculty and administrative negotiation, with give and take on both sides. The resultant package moves us well toward the goal of raising the status of teaching, with faculty being given much greater control over their own progress through the system. The caveats to keep information flowing and to get feedback, and more feedback, were especially valuable here. Several sensitive issues (the importance of student feedback to faculty evaluation being a good example) sparked great concern and fueled many rumors. It was fairly late in the process before we finally realized the need to increase our efforts at communicating each development as fast as possible. Although ending well, there were some touchy moments. Once again, a retreat was a key strategy. One hundred Miami-Dade persons and ten outside guests came together to review preliminary proposals. Their recommendations, forcefully (often painfully, from the committee's perspective) delivered, resulted in a drastic redraft and improvement. It is almost certain that without the benefit of those extra points of view, the referendum would have had a very different outcome.

The capstone of the college's faculty advancement plan is the Endowed Teaching Chairs Program. Unlike university chairs, these will be awarded to faculty on the basis of teaching excellence. Chairs will be held for three years, and only those who have been in a faculty role at Miami-Dade for six consecutive years prior to nomination will be eligible. The intent, clearly, is to recognize those who have given excellent performance on behalf of Miami-Dade students. To date, forty chairs have been endowed, although none have been awarded. Nor will any be awarded until criteria and selection procedures have been carefully worked out. These, along with the other components of faculty advancement, will be derived in large part from the statement of faculty excellence.

The remaining recommendations will build on those already adopted. Before the project is done, both administrators and support staff will have statements of excellence and policies and procedures tying their advancement to their own excellence. That we did not foresee involving all college personnel in the project earlier was an error, but not a fatal one. "The project that ate Miami-Dade," as the president has come to refer to it, is progressing well.

Bringing About Significant Change

The following components are critical to the success of a major institutional effort to improve teaching and learning:

1. *A Commitment from the Top.* Significant change simply does not happen unless the people who work in an institution understand that the chief executive officer and the

college's leadership are committed to that change. The commitment needs to be demonstrated by actions as well as by words. At Miami-Dade Community College, the president proposed the project; serves on, and is in attendance at, all steering committee meetings and retreats; and personally has held more than fifty small-group meetings with faculty during the project's course to discuss process and to get feedback. He has taken action to see that the recommendations coming out of subcommittees, once adopted, are in fact implemented. Many of these involved significant adjustment. To illustrate, for 1989-90, the four campuses in combination will have just under a million-dollar budget for teaching-learning resource centers. These funds will come from administrative reductions and shifting of priorities from other programs to staff and program development.

2. *Provision for an Evolving Process.* In anything as far reaching and complex as the Teaching-Learning Project, no one person or small group of persons will ever have all the good ideas or think of all contingencies. Some good ideas will work, some will not. It is important to have a plan that moves along, but the plan must leave room for contributions to be made along the way. There must be the kind of interaction that provides for midcourse adjustments in direction, and new emphases, reexamination of and change in original thinking. That the best view of reality is the one coming from multiple perspectives may be a cliché, but it is nonetheless true. A project is strengthened as assumptions are opened to examination, put to the test of multiple views, and adjusted as new ideas are brought into the process. At the beginning of this project, we had no idea that so much focus would be needed on administrative behavior or that support staff would be so anxious to become a part of the process, to cite two examples.

3. *Shared Ownership.* As essential as it may be that the chief executive demonstrate commitment, it must not be seen as that individual's project. As many as feasible must have the opportunity to become directly involved, to see their views attended to, and to review the ideas of others. There

must be a broad ownership of outcomes, especially ones that will affect the way individuals work, the nature of the institution, and the way people are compensated. If there is an overused word (but not an overused concept) in the Miami-Dade project, it is *feedback*. Surveys have been used extensively and results been incorporated; one-on-one interviews and numerous small-group meetings have been conducted; the president has initiated several series of small-group meetings at key stages in the process. There was also a workshop with the district board of trustees and two retreats (with more to come).

We have known from the early stages of the project that the goals toward which we are working cannot be reached without substantial commitment from large numbers of faculty and staff. Making sure people know what is going on is critical before asking for their commitment. Even so, in a few instances an opportunity to keep constituents informed was sacrificed as we concentrated on finishing some component of a proposal. This type of action always had negative consequences. Had the occurrence been common, it might have proved damaging. Putting the advancement subcommittee proposals to the test of a faculty referendum was a clear request for commitment and a test of how well we had set the stage with our colleagues. If we were politicians, we might describe the result of the referendum as a mandate to proceed with the program. We might offer the results as evidence that, although we were not doing everything right, we had a good product that was widely understood.

4. *A Solid Research Base.* It is important to utilize research techniques in garnering information from within the institution. In addition, on many of the key issues we were examining, other institutions had studied, postulated, and tried ideas. It made sense for us to build on the base of what others had learned. There are many instances where standing on the shoulders of those who came before is appropriate.

5. *Outside Expertise.* As we become involved in any task, interact continually with our own colleagues, and shape major decisions, it is certainly possible to overlook some very

important details. Stopping periodically in the early stages to have individuals from outside the institution view one's work is important and often enlightening. One example will make the case. During the retreat on faculty excellence, one of our outside consultants observed that we had made a strong case for the importance of faculty giving time to students, of treating students with respect, and of evaluating their teaching techniques. We had, however, omitted all reference to the importance of academic competence and preparation. We were all stunned by our collective oversight. The retreat had been preceded by over a year of committee work and two rounds of surveys; still, we had missed that key element.

6. *Training and Support.* If there has been a common thread in the recommendations emerging from subcommittee work, it is the importance of training. The more divergent a proposed change is from current practice, the more strongly was the need for training prior to implementation emphasized. We expect faculty to be able to turn to an institution for support to improve instruction; however, particularly heavy emphasis was placed on training for department chairs, associate deans, and deans. We believe the provision for a year of training prior to implementation of new faculty advancement policies contributed to the positive referendum outcome by helping to overcome a natural resistance to change. If an institution is going to ask a lot, it also must make clear that it is willing to give a lot in exchange for effort.

7. *Patience.* The college is now nearing completion of three years of work on the Teaching-Learning Project. At least one year of development remains and probably two to three years of implementation. The impact will be pervasive; the institution will be better and very different at the conclusion of this work. To have the best possible products developed, to have all pieces fit, to get widespread commitment, to encourage behavior change, and to go through the process of adjusting budgets, patience and a long-term view are required. It will seem rather daring for a chief executive officer to embark on a seven-year program when the average ten-

ure of a president of a community college is three to five years. However Miami-Dade Community College has had the stability from the board and its administrative personnel to take on this kind of project.

Finally, it is important to note that there will be setbacks, there will be doubters and there will be those who are disinterested, skeptical concerning motives, and entrenched in the status quo. If one really believes in the project, one will need perseverance, dedication, and commitment to achieve substantive change. And if one succeeds, there can be advances beyond expectations, enthusiastic supporters, rebirth of interest in the teaching profession, rededication of energy, affirmations of trust, and an excitement about the future and about being part of an institution that is striving to make a real contribution to education in this nation.

CHAPTER 11

Summary and Recommendations for Academic Leaders
Peter Seldin

This book has offered a broad range of strategies for achieving the climate and support needed for effective teaching in colleges and universities, specifically spelling out the special role of academic leaders in fostering high-quality teaching. Below follow chapter-by-chapter key points and recommendations for how administrators can effect needed changes for spreading teaching excellence throughout the institution.

Chapter One

1. In academic life today, teaching is widely undervalued. The approach seems to be to talk about the importance of teaching but to evaluate faculty primarily on the basis of scholarly achievements and professional activities.
2. To bring a new professionalism to teaching requires a new campus climate that supports and rewards effective teaching and accords it equal status with scholarly research and publication.
3. If colleges and universities are going to embrace superior

teachers and superior scholars equally, the initiative and guidance for such transformation must come from administrative leaders, who must champion the idea and personally crusade for its importance.

4. This positive rhetoric supporting teaching must be accompanied by supportive institutional policies and practices instigated by administrators.

5. Experience suggests that five approaches, used in combination, work well for giving teaching a higher priority: (1) making the campus environment more responsive to teaching, (2) providing a congenial background and the necessary tools for teaching, (3) assisting graduate students to develop teaching skills, (4) offering appropriate rewards for superior teaching, and (5) introducing an effective faculty development system.

6. Professors can document their classroom performance by using the teaching portfolio, a relatively new method that has an impressive track record. The teaching portfolio contains all the documents and materials that collectively reflect the scope and quality of the professor's teaching performance. The portfolio is to teaching what lists of publications, grants, and honors are to research and scholarship.

Chapter Two

1. Institutional conditions make a significant difference to teaching performance. The organizational environment shapes faculty attitudes, perceptions, and performance for better or worse.

2. Administrative leaders have a major affect on institutional conditions, which in turn influence faculty morale and motivation to teach.

3. The key organizational characteristics supporting faculty morale and motivation to teach are (1) a distinctive organizational culture, (2) a participatory leadership, (3) organizational momentum, (4) a formal faculty development program, and (5) a broader view of scholarship.

4. At liberal arts colleges, where teaching is central to the institutional mission, faculty morale is closely linked to incentives motivating faculty to take teaching seriously. In contrast, at research universities, faculty morale and motivation to teach are not necessarily correlated. In fact, efforts to encourage serious attention to teaching may actually increase tensions and diminish morale.

5. In motivating research university faculty to take teaching seriously, three factors are critical. First, as in smaller colleges, teaching must be a strongly valued institutional commitment. Second, administrative leaders must take a public stand on the importance of teaching and support this stand with initiatives on incentives to motivate faculty to value teaching. Third, universities interested in promoting teaching excellence will gain reciprocal benefit from creating communities of faculty that share that commitment.

6. Destabilizing faculty morale and motivation to teach is the gap between the institutional mission and what professors are actually rewarded for doing. Professors are heliotropic and respond to the incentives offered by the institution.

Chapter Three

1. Deans, chairs, and academic vice-presidents are king makers who can make things happen on campus. They can plant ideas, nurture them, solicit support from faculty leaders for them, and nudge them through often tortuous dialogue and revision until they are ultimately "owned" by the affected groups.

2. Good teaching is a motherhood-and-apple-pie issue—no one is against it. The problems affecting good teaching are inertia, overcoming fear of change, and the fact that faculty priorities may be elsewhere.

3. Symbolic gestures need to be accompanied by concrete action if culture is to change. Making good teaching an institutional priority requires changing values, behaviors, and academic norms.

4. Creating a more favorable climate requires the public articulation, forcefully and repeatedly, of the new values and priorities. Convocations, faculty meetings, and retreats for various groups are important methods for leveraging change.
5. Since faculty are often disposed to disparage and resist administrative leadership, academic administrators must seriously listen to faculty about how to accomplish change and must be prepared, within reason, to follow faculty recommendations.
6. Institutional strategies to elevate the importance of teaching include: (1) making good teaching a leadership priority for administrators; (2) encouraging faculty dialogue across disciplines and participation in conferences and workshops focusing on teaching excellence; (3) viewing teaching as involving students, the public, and encompassing scholarship broadly defined; (4) making teaching ability a criterion for hiring new faculty; and (5) rewarding good teaching both in word and deed.

Chapter Four

1. No one is in a better position than the department chair to nurture a climate in which teaching is accorded high value and in which faculty members can deepen their understanding about the learning process and about which teaching strategies are effective under which conditions.
2. The department chair wields a special power to enhance teaching effectiveness and needs to be aware of strategies for bringing about that enhancement.
3. Among the interventions available to the chair are (1) creating a climate of trust and support in which visiting each other's classrooms is considered acceptable; (2) requiring all applicants for faculty positions to make presentations to faculty and students prior to faculty appointment; (3) rewarding good teaching with money, public recognition, and positive reinforcement; (4) discussing

the many aspects of teaching at department meetings and workshops; (5) building a department library on teaching; (6) introducing a mentoring system in which two faculty members work together as a team of teacher and observer.

4. The department chair can foster collaboration, create win-win resolutions, and promote integrative solutions to problems. The chair can thank professors for suggestions and acknowledge their personal value. And the chair can be generous in recognizing professors, often through sharing of the credit for any project's success.

5. The department chair has the potential to be the most effective agent for change. To realize that potential, however, the chair requires empowerment, knowledge, and skills. The chair needs training in the skills of leadership and empowerment derived from the broad support of deans and vice-presidents for academic affairs.

Chapter Five

1. One of the most important actions an academic administrator can take to improve teaching is to assess it accurately and to reward it when effective. To say that the institution values teaching when in reality it rewards research and scholarship is not a credible message.

2. Categorizing teaching performance as "needs improvement" does not necessarily mean that the teaching is deficient; it simply means that it is not perfect. A professor can move from B level, a strong performance, to A level, a stronger performance.

3. Student ratings are best used as one of a number of sources of data about a professor's teaching. The ratings correlate reasonably well with measures of student learning and with ratings of administrators, faculty colleagues, self-ratings, alumni ratings and the ratings of trained observers. Student rating systems should be flexible, provide comparative data, control for bias, and be diagnostic and easily interpretable.

4. Teaching materials—including handouts, the syllabus, exams, graded essays, even lecture notes—provide useful information on such aspects of a professor's teaching as course design, curriculum development, and mastery of the subject matter.

5. Classroom observation techniques, when combined with videotaping or even audiotaping, provide a permanent record of what took place in the classroom. These approaches also enable the professor to distance him- or herself and observe performance in a more objective, detached way.

6. Teachers should be encouraged to look for the positive aspects of the performance, not just those areas in need of improvement. It is unfortunate that academics tend, when receiving a score of ninety-seven on a test, to focus on the three-point error. The use of the negative approach in assessing teaching virtually ensures that the process will be counterproductive. Teachers need to be made aware of their strengths as well as their shortcomings.

Chapter Six

1. Faculty evaluation is often a contentious issue. Part of the problem results from faculty concern that evaluative information intended to improve teaching may end up being used by administrators for personnel review. That concern can be eliminated by placing the evaluative information under the control of the instructor.

2. To improve instruction, it is not enough to have information of a general kind, such as summary ratings of teaching. Instead, information must be specific and diagnostic and must identify what needs changing and offer corrective suggestions.

3. To guide evaluation, a model is needed that distinguishes among major components of the instructional process and suggests what information is appropriate for diagnosing and strengthening each component. Such a model is the four Ps model of instruction, the components of

which include preconditions, plans, procedures, and products. Each component of the four Ps model can distinctively contribute to solving instructional problems.

4. Although the leading role in improving instruction is played by the teacher, administrators have an important supporting role. For example, administrators can establish lunchtime conversations on teaching; create a collection of books, articles, and videotapes and place them in the faculty lounge; make sure that each new faculty member has a mentor during the first year at the institution; and expect each teacher to report formally each year on improvements in at least one course.

5. Administrators should create a climate in which instructional evaluation is expected and should cultivate norms that encourage faculty to invest time and energy in instructional improvement. They should ensure that rewards for effective teaching are frequent and generous.

Chapter Seven

1. To have an impact on the quality of education, administrators need to give some attention to three qualities of educational leadership. Leadership must be (1) perceived as vitally interested in and supportive of all efforts by everyone to improve teaching and learning; (2) knowledgeable about what constitutes educational excellence, specifically what makes teaching good for students and satisfying for teachers; and (3) willing to provide incentives and rewards to move faculty and administrators toward excellence in teaching and learning.

2. Teachers should assume more personal responsibility for what is taught and learned in their classrooms. One way to do this is to involve teachers in classroom research, the systematic and insightful observation about how students learn a particular subject matter.

3. The ultimate goal of classroom research is to make teaching more productive—to close the gap between what is taught and what is learned. The premise of classroom

research is that by monitoring what students are learning, teachers can know more about their teaching effectiveness.

4. As the area of classroom research matures, there is also established a close relationship with faculty development. This relationship has the potential for a strong bond, since both share the same goal: to make teaching more professional and based on understanding, insights, knowledge, and skills.

5. Administrators should provide and support opportunities for teachers to engage in classroom research, both individually and in small groups of interested and motivated faculty, and should use the results for departmental improvement and evaluation. They should also promote local discussions of classroom research projects, affording those who teach an opportunity to share designs and findings and to receive local recognition for participation in professional development.

Chapter Eight

1. The bond between state institutions and state government is often a bond that chafes. Public cooperation and unity often mask tensions between autonomy and accountability. Administrators must understand the state's role and its potential for providing leadership and resources in improving teaching. They must also be aware how to use state offices to encourage faculty and student learning.

2. State government has three levers influencing the quality of higher education: rhetoric, initiatives, and regulation. State officials tend to seize center stage in setting the agenda for higher education and defining the terms of improvement. They pursue a tactical rather than a collaborative approach to issues.

3. The best strategy for college and university administrators is to take the offensive, to articulate their own regional and intrainstitutional agendas and recommendations for change. This is particularly important to counter state agendas emphasizing research and graduate education.

4. Both student assessment and state "centers of excellence" programs offer potent possibilities for strengthening undergraduate teaching. The possibilities increase when administrators maximize control over what is presented to the state as assessment results, and funding proposals.

5. For excellence in undergraduate teaching, administrators must establish institutional priorities and allocate resources. These priorities may run counter to state funding guidelines. Institutional discretion may be granted if stout, even confrontational, opposition is maintained.

Chapter Nine

1. How teaching is reviewed and how its value to the institution is determined are vital questions to administrators. The time is overdue for institutions to scrutinize the methods by which faculty classroom performance is reviewed and strengthened. Excellence in teaching should be placed on an equal plane with excellence in scholarly productivity.

2. Administrators should sponsor faculty teaching presentations. These presentations can be on a particular professor's research project or on teaching issues.

3. Administrators should strengthen the perception of the importance of teaching by making it more visible to the community. They should also support campuswide discussions on the relationship between what is known and what is taught.

4. A faculty committee should be charged with the development of educational topics for discussion each year. Off-campus speakers should be invited.

5. The preparation of graduate teaching assistants and the initiation of new faculty should include demonstrations of student learning differences, to which all faculty are invited. The demonstrations should identify differences originating not only in gender, race, and ethnic background but also in such physical disabilities as dyslexia.

Chapter Ten

1. Teaching and learning are the heart of an educational institution. Every institutional activity therefore affects teaching and learning, and every institutional effort to improve teaching must engage the entire college or university. Miami-Dade Community College (M-DCC) is a case in point. This college accepted the challenge to improve teaching and went on to sweeping changes in institutional practices.

2. M-DCC has upended the way it does business. Its highest priority is now the improvement of teaching and learning, and the entire faculty reward system rests on classroom performance.

3. These changes have been accomplished because faculty members firmly believe that the president and other leading administrators are committed in word and deed to teaching excellence.

4. These changes have evolved over three years. At the start, M-DCC committed itself to take as long as necessary for substantial numbers of faculty to be persuaded and brought into the process. Subcommittees were set to work, continuous feedback was sought and obtained on proposed changes, written surveys and small-group meetings were used. Outside experts were brought in. In addition, there was a two-day, off-campus retreat and several mid-course adjustments in direction and emphasis.

5. To make effective teaching an institutional priority does not happen easily. There are doubters and nay sayers and others who could not care less. Some are suspicious of motives and others resist change. To wear down resistance over time by persuasion and example requires a persevering and dedicated administration. The price is worth it.

A Final Word

Any book devoted to improving college and university teaching must not overlook the vital dimension of how new faculty members are prepared for their roles as teachers. The topic has been touched on in a number of chapters but not discussed in depth.

The problem of preparing college teachers is not new. It was succinctly reported at a conference held in 1949: "The American college teacher is the only high-level professional man (or woman) . . . who enters upon a career with neither the prerequisite trial of competence nor experience in the use of the tools of his (or her) profession" (Blegen and Cooper, 1950, p. 123). This reproachful judgment is almost as valid today as it was forty years ago. Despite much discussion over the years and fitful evidence of increased interest in the problem, the graduate school experience still focuses on graduate study and research, and graduate students are provided only skimpy preparation for teaching.

If college and university teaching are to be improved, graduate schools must introduce effective programs for preparing teachers. There is no alternative. The fact is, the typical graduate school program fails in several ways. It does not help the new teacher identify and develop a style of teaching well suited to his or her strengths and interests. It does not develop the kind of perspective the new teacher needs to deal with the differences and range of motivations among the students in a class. It does not help the new teacher select subject matter and sequence it in a fashion appropriate to the courses the new teacher will teach (Wise, 1967; Seldin, 1988). In short, graduate students may have fine-tuned their research skills by the time they earn their doctorates, but many are uninformed about teaching.

That is perhaps why the Association of American Colleges is embarked on a three-year project to emphasize teaching and other professional issues related to faculty careers. Graduate students at three doctoral-granting institutions will visit with faculty members at nearby liberal arts colleges. They will also take two seminars—one devoted to teaching, advising, and governance, the other to teaching subjects in their disciplines.

Graduate education, in addition to preparing students to do research, should also prepare students to teach. Graduate students, including those who are *not* teaching assistants, should be given structured opportunities to observe excellent teachers using different modes of instruction, to teach under supervision, and to benefit from an analysis of good and bad teaching, including their own. Close attention should be paid to the theoretical and practical analyses of curriculum and course construction, evaluation of different teaching techniques, and the development of teaching styles. All students should have the opportunity during their graduate education to participate directly in various forms of teaching. They should not be restricted to supervising laboratory work or grading papers but should lead discussions, lectures, use cases, make demonstrations and simulations—all under supervision. Additionally, graduate education should lead to an understanding of different ethnic and cultural backgrounds and the ways in which different individuals value and approach the learning experience. Age, gender, educational background, and learning styles should be given due consideration (Andrews, 1985; Seldin, 1988; Nyquist, Abbott, and Wulff, 1989).

Teaching Assistant Training. At most institutions the training of teaching assistants is only marginally less rudimentary than that of nonteaching assistants, but interest in improving preparation seems to be rising. More than 500 participants, most of them graduate school administrators or instructors in teaching assistant training programs, attended the Second National Conference on the Training and Employment of Teaching Assistants in November 1989. The *Chronicle of Higher Education* (see Monaghan, 1989) reported some sobering facts that were discussed at the conference:

- Campuswide training programs operate in only 25 percent of the institutions that use teaching assistants.
- Only half of all academic departments provide training to teaching assistants, and few follow up to improve their teaching skills.
- Many institutions simply assume teaching assistants can teach and do not concern themselves with such matters as whether they have an aptitude for or interest in teaching.

- Some institutions have almost as many teaching assistants as faculty members.

All too often, teaching assistant preparation is little more than a summer orientation program lasting a week or, in many cases, a single day. If it is to be useful, teaching assistant preparation must be continuous; orientation should be followed by consultation, monitoring, and workshops. Teaching assistants should be introduced step by step to more complex teaching tasks over several years. Strategies for improving teaching, such as videotaping, peer observation, and student ratings, should be integrated into every teaching assistant program.

Who should provide the training? Weimer, Svinicki, and Bauer (1989) suggest four possibilities: (1) training can be offered by the instructional/faculty development unit of the university; (2) training can occur within the department to which the teaching assistant is assigned; (3) specialized training can take place at the level of a single course run by a coordinator for all teaching assistants teaching that course and covering, for example, teaching, content, and assignments; or (4) training can be provided by the graduate school or the institution. Most of the time, teacher assistant training is offered through a combination of these approaches.

Administrators' Role in Teaching Assistant Training. University administrators who carry general responsibility for the quality of undergraduate teaching are, unfortunately, rarely involved in the selection of teaching assistants or in the development of activities to help them improve their teaching ability. Similarly, academic vice-presidents, deans, and department chairs in undergraduate colleges often have little or no contact with the teaching assistant program. Only recently have some academic administrators begun to address themselves to this aspect of life, probably the result of mounting public pressure.

Academic administrators face the need for more thoughtful and continuous leadership, if teaching assistant programs are to be restructured so as to genuinely prepare future professors to teach. What can academic administrators be expected to do? First, they should use the power of office to make clear to faculty and students, and to the public at large, their personal support of training programs. They should smooth the path, sell the idea, proffer financial assistance, and clothe training programs with legitimacy. They should offer initiatives. They should involve directors of teaching assistant programs in setting ambitious but realistic goals, implementing them, and evaluating successes and failures (Andrews, 1985; Seldin, 1988). In short, administrators should see to it that teaching assistant programs are characterized by progressively heavier teaching responsibilities in a supervised and supportive environment. This will truly be a major service to their institutions and to generations of future teachers.

References

Andrews, J.D.W. (ed.). *Strengthening the Teaching Assistant Faculty.* New Directions for Teaching and Learning, no. 22. San Francisco: Jossey-Bass, 1985.

Blegen, T., and Cooper, R. (eds.). *The Preparation of Teachers.* Washington: American Council on Education, 1950.

Monaghan, P. "University Officials Deplore the Lack of Adequate Training Given to Teaching Assistants, Ponder How to Improve It." *Chronicle of Higher Education,* Nov. 29, 1989, p. A17.

Nyquist, J. D., Abbott, R. D., and Wulff, D. H. (eds.). *Teaching Assistant Training in the 1990s.* New Directions for Teaching and Learning, no. 39. San Francisco: Jossey-Bass, 1989.

Seldin, P. "Academic Culture." Paper presented at the International Conference on New Concepts in Higher Education, Bangkok, Thailand, Dec. 1988.

Weimer, M., Svinicki, M. D., and Bauer, G. "Designing Programs to Prepare TAs to Teach." In J. D. Nyquist, R. D. Abbott, and D. H. Wulff (eds.), *Teaching Assistant Training in the 1990s.* New Directions for Teaching and Learning, no. 39. San Francisco: Jossey-Bass, 1989.

Wise, W. M. "Who Teaches the Teachers?" In C.B.T. Lee (ed.), *Improving College Teaching*. Washington, D.C.: American Council on Education, 1967.

Index